I WANT YOU TO MEET

MY JESUS

THE CONVERSION OF AN OLD BARN

By
Roger Hosking MBE

Dedications

Brenda Cotton - A gracious lady who was the first in Etwall to talk about the Holy Spirit and who cried a lot of tears at the rejection of the same. But for us, she was a gentle warrior who often corrected us but above all told us to write everything down – without that advice and the many diaries and notes over thirty-eight years this book would not have been possible.

(January 2021 - Since writing that dedication Brenda has passed away)

I would like to add further dedications to:

Sam and Karen - A lovely couple who have loved us and supported us in many ways. They are directors of Betel and manage the Etwall project and have taken over our vision. They are the answer to the prophecy we received long ago *"we would build it and others would run it."*

One dark cold night as I was shutting the hens up and going through a period of depression, there came an arm over my shoulder "Are you OK mate?" "No" was my reply "I feel I have failed badly." "No you haven't, without you, I wouldn't be with my wife Karen or had my amazing little boy Daniel." I had been touched by an angel and all felt different.

David Hales - A true British gentleman who came to us in the late 1990s, volunteering as a qualified 'special needs' teacher. He transformed the way we did things and was responsible for the respect we received from the schools that used us.

He chose to raise the money in 2000 to build a classroom that I said, "we didn't need". He was a teacher to the students and a very dear friend and prayer partner until we closed down in 2019 and then sadly he passed away in 2021.

Acknowledgements

I will never read a book in the same way again having now realised how many people have been part of and helped to create the story and then the book. There are so many to whom I am so grateful. I am very thankful for all of you.

Jim and Cynthia Wilkinson and "Miracle Valley" for introducing us to the Holy Spirit, for being available on the phone for over 30 years through some of my worst times.

Christopher and Christine Bacon, who have been consistent and wonderful spiritual friends from the beginning with support and often hard advice.

Jim Hadfield, who in 1984 said "I will be in the Barn to pray on Saturday at 8am." The Barn had no roof but it did not rain at that time of day for two years. The prayer meeting continued at different times until 2019.

Alan Davenport. In 1995 a land rover appeared regularly. A stranger came to walk his dog. We then got to know that stranger. He was a retired teacher and came to us as a volunteer working with the students and stayed with us particularly as a prayer partner until 2020.

David Hales, who transformed a rough farm project into a professional place of education.

Pam and David Watson. What a team!. They developed a huge egg ministry and we all queued up wanting to make their delivery - 180 dozen. Happy Hens and it's ministry were well known in the Ashby area. David sadly passed away but Pam has continued to be an amazing support and spent many hours "editing" this book..

Finally, Beryl and the children. Beryl's creative gifts have put the icing on the cake and made this place so special and to the children whose lives were upended and survived!

Endorsements

"I count it a privilege and honour to pen these words of commendation and thanksgiving on behalf of my friends Roger and Beryl Hosking. The sharing of their journey over the decades has been by telephone and several times when meeting together.

Roger has written many 'memory notes' throughout his journey with its daily hills and valleys which he and his family have encountered; the unknown territory we call tomorrow, now unfolded. May you who dare to read the whole story be challenged, encouraged and thankful to keep walking forward with your journey, **with your best friend Jesus."**

Jim Wilkinson
Hollybush Christian Fellowship (Miracle Valley)

"Roger has a heart of gold, a love for the unlovable and a passion to tell everyone about Jesus. He and Beryl have given their lives helping vulnerable young people. Their story is both enriching and heart breaking. It is very moving. The faith and perseverance they have shown is an example to all of the power of prayer and what can be achieved when we keep on pushing through. Well done!"

David and Di Harper,
Top Barn Farm, Worcestershire.

Foreword

It was almost too late when I realised I had had a wonderful father. My mum left home when I was five which left me badly hurting emotionally. My dad did the best he could, but he could never by my mum. I was sent to boarding school at ten years old and continued to be a 'problem'. However during the last four years of his life I had the privilege of looking after my dad. This was a very precious time.

My story that you are about to read is the transition from a broken, hurting child to a responsible, loving adult. The message of my life is this; no matter how bad things are or seem to be Jesus can change any life if He is invited to. All you have to do is ask Him in.

During the course of my life I have been involved with young people who have never heard of Jesus. I have gotten frustrated at times when I cannot convince them and yet I have sown a seed for the Lord as He has told me to. A farmer or a gardener would never expect to sow the seed and reap the harvest in the same season,

"see how the farmer waits for the land to yield its valuable crop and how patient he is for the autumn and spring

rains." James 5:7 (NIV). So with this verse in mind I am happy to be a part of the Lord's building process.

Those who know about the barn at Etwall could be forgiven for thinking that a lot happened in a very short time. Certainly, a lot did happen since the building and restoration work started in December 1985. At that time, many people said, "Where would all the money, materials and help come from?" Various estimates were made from £20,000 to £40,000. This was for the first part of the barn. Before the work went ahead we came to realise that God's biggest problem was 'US'. For us, the greatest moves were long before the building started.

This introduction was written in 1988 and refers to the previous eight years.

I have read many books and heard many stories of the wonderful miraculous ways in which God has worked to create and build and change. Over the years I have found them quite depressing because I have wondered why have they not happened to me?

As we read the stories of the Old Testament characters we see that they went through long periods of building in their own lives before God used them in the work He had for them. So it is with modern day stories. I hope you will forgive me if I relate our search and struggles, mistakes, and failures because I believe they are the foundations to the barn and will be of help and encouragement to anyone who is longing to serve God and yet are wondering why He does not use them.

Contents

Introduction

Why Am I Writing This Book?

The reason why I am writing this book and presumably why you are reading it, is simply this, "I want you to meet my Jesus."

My dad always had a picture on his office wall. Jesus is knocking on the door, there is no handle on the outside of the door, the handle is on the inside so that the only one who can open the door is the one on the inside and so it is with you and I we are the ones who can let Him in. My Jesus has been with me all the way. He has protected me and has heard my cry. He has allowed me to get into trouble, has broken His heart over me and even died for me! Even though things may have often gone badly wrong, He has always been there. The truth is that up to recently I had wanted Him to be like Father Christmas. I wanted Him to give me what I want but I had not let Him into my heart and allowed Him to call the shots.

There is a painting on the ceiling of the Sistine Chapel by Michelangelo – God is on a cloud, His finger is reaching out, His arm outstretched and His index finger straight. His gaze is fixed on Adam. He is getting as close as He can to Adam. Adam's posture is different. He is very relaxed, arm relaxed and finger slightly bent. There is a small gap between the end of Adam's finger and the end of God's finger. God is desperate to reach us. Yet we are relaxed. It's up to us to make the final move.

We all have got a picture
Built up in our mind's eye
Of who or what our God is
Right up there in the sky.

Some say He is a kindly man
With hair all long and brown
And some an older friendly face
His hand is reaching down.

But He is not up there above
He's right here down below
His hand enfolds us all the while
His Peace and strength is now.

So, like a child have faith in Him
Relax and let Him lead

> You day by day in work and play,
> He'll fill your every need.

This book has been written over many years by myself, a man of 79 with fifty years of memories. I have taken many excerpts from my diaries written over the years. I have included some of those excerpts word for word as that is how my story and faith grew. My hope is that from it you will come to understand my story and the journey I travelled with My Jesus throughout my life. My first notes for this book are dated 1984 and it is now 1988 **(actually 2022!!)** and although the story will go on (and for the barn hopefully) until my life on earth is over. I wanted to record my search and how I saw things as a young Christian for other new Christians to read and find encouragement.

January 2021 - Some time ago

It's several years since I started writing this book and my diaries go back to 1984. So much has happened since then. On the face of it much of it seems bad but looking back and seeing the hand of God in it all, we can see answered prayer more than we could ever hope for or imagine. It is quite hard to understand why God can allow things to go wrong or in fact why I should expect someone to want to meet my Jesus, but those times would have been unimaginable without Him. He said *"I will never leave you or forsake you.*

My child I will never let go of your hand," and that is the key to wanting you to meet Him so He can be with you too.

I am a fanatical reader of both Christian books and fiction and much of who I am today has come from reading books. But right now I need to say the answer is not in a book, not this book, as all our stories are different, but all answers can be found in the Bible. You do not need to "look" for Him as he is right there beside you now. He longs to take you in His arms but you have to invite Him, you have to open the door. In my story you will find that I made many commitments. Nothing seemed to change. I have worked with so many broken people and seen them make commitments and often nothing changed. The key is this, we want God to come into our lives but on our terms. We do not want to change but we want the blessing, like Father Christmas turning up at Christmas to give us what we want.

I was eighteen years old when I went forward at a meeting at Spicer Street Baptist Church in St Albans. I was forty two years old when in a prayer meeting in our lounge at the farm I started to cry. Someone had died, but who? Then I realised it was me, I had been born again!

Needless to say a lot happened between starting this book on 7th November 2009 and January

2012. A lot happened to me between eighteen years old and forty two years old. I am now seventy nine and still being overawed at what God can do, through the good times and more importantly the bad times.

It is now January 2021, 2020, has just ended and was possibly the worst year anyone can imagine. It started with my step-mum Elaine dying. She was dearly loved by many and described as 'liquid gold'. Actually her death was somewhat of a blessing because at ninety two years old she had become very frail. Shortly after her funeral Covid19 arrived and it would have been hard looking after her. Funerals were a major problem at that time too with the country sent into a lockdown. She is now with my dad, and one day I will be with her again.

The farm had been for sale for three years and as I write today over a year later another 1,400 people will die today from Covid and we are locked down again. Churches are closed and we know of so many who are suffering from loneliness, depression, and dementia.

"Why Lord?" No matter how well you get to know my Jesus, we will always have questions like these. Some we may come to understand and yet when there is no definable answer we trust and bask in His love knowing that He is constantly with us in every circumstance and the trials we face and ultimately we will one day meet Him face-to-face in Glory.

It has taken me 37 years to write this, so bless you for reading my story I really do want you to meet my Jesus.

ITS BEEN AN INCREDIBLE JOURNEY!

Chapter I

In the Beginning

In 1984 Beryl and I were quite 'normal'. I was a steward at the local church; and Beryl was a Sunday School teacher. We had a 100acre farm that was not very successful and a big house.

You could say we were 'Sunday Christians'. We had met at the Queen's Hall Methodist Mission in Derby but moved to the Etwall Methodist Church when we got married in 1978. I guess we wanted something more and got involved with Youth for Christ in Derby and in particular John, who was the leader at that time. The meetings were a real eye opener. People with their hands raised in the air, dancing in the aisle and generally doing things that frankly made us feel uncomfortable, but they had such a look of love on their faces, and at the end of the meetings people were prayed for and we couldn't dispute it, PEOPLE GOT HEALED!

And then it happened. John said to us "My God's alive. I am sorry to hear about yours!!" Well you don't say that kind of thing to a Methodist steward do you? But rather than be offended we had to admit that John took his Bible seriously and believed every word. Wherever he went he expected things to happen. And they did!

At that time we read a book called "Miracle Valley" written by a farmer called Jim Wilkinson. He was Methodist preacher but quite a unique one. He and Cynthia had encountered the Holy Spirit, had had some amazing experiences and were finally 'born again', a saying that at that time meant nothing to us. But life was just beginning for them and again people were being healed.

Reading through our diaries, it could have been suggested that 1984 was a year in which we should really have given up and yet it was the year everything started. This could also be said of 1990 and 2010/11. For those were the years that without Jesus and much prayer, things would have been impossible.

My Story

I was born in 1942 during the blitz in London. I am told that I was evacuated to Wales as the war was ending. When they came to fetch me I had disappeared. At the end of Sandringham Gardens was a football stadium turned into a pig farm for the war. That is where they found me, a budding farmer at three years old.

At that time we were a normal family, mum, and dad, me and two brothers. My dad was a committed Christian and spent the war as a conscientious objector and had lost his job as a result. Then my mum left home when I was five years old and everything changed. I changed from being a normal kid to being a big problem.

After the war dad worked away a lot in America and Africa. He was becoming famous in his profession as a consulting actuary (pension funds). Among other things he started the Stock Exchange in Nigeria and wrote an annual book for Bank Managers entitled 'Hosking on Pensions'. Dad employed housekeepers to look after us, whom my brothers and I drove out with the ferocity of a house dog. I was often sent to my bedroom, but my brothers would get a ladder to get me out. Each time dad returned home he had to find another Housekeeper!

At ten years old I had driven my dad ragged. He was not a bad dad and in fact looking back, I would say he was a brilliant dad, but no matter how hard he tried he could not be my mum. This had a huge impact on my life's future. Like so many youngsters today who too are growing up without their mum or dad around. I was not a bad kid I was a hurting kid. Despite that, there was something happening inside of me.

Every year we had a traditional Christmas. On Christmas Day all the relatives came to us and we had presents and too much to eat, then on Boxing Day we went to my uncle Eric's house and once again there were more presents and too much to eat. He lived in the heart of London and although the war had ended some years previously there were a lot of derelict bomb sites. As we passed one it was easy to see, even to one as young as I was, that there were people living on those bomb sites – poorly clothed, hungry, and only a cardboard box for shelter. "Where would Jesus be today daddy?" I asked. Poor dad had no answer to that and even now it still tells me I am in the wrong place on Christmas Day.

In 1952 I was sent off to boarding school. I didn't like school and school didn't like me. The regular punishment was a rubber slipper on my *'bare bum'*, and I spent a lot of time not being able to sit down properly. When dad died I found a file about me with several letters from my headmaster one of which said, "Society needs to be protected from people like Roger." I was not a bad kid I was a hurting kid, and the more I was punished the naughtier I became. Later on God was to give me a vision to work with broken people, with a deep understanding of how they felt. They needed to be loved just like I did. More than that, they needed to know the love of Jesus.

At school I was quite badly bullied, afraid of my own shadow and very insecure. I used to have a recurring dream of walking on a huge rotten wooden floor. Wherever I put my foot the floor broke, so I had to keep moving and was unable to rest. I know now that a very special hand kept lifting me up.

What little I knew of church then was a rather boring building and a lot of boring people Once a week at school we had 'Religious Education.' In those days it was pure Christianity. Our teacher was a little old lady. Her class was thirty or so rebellious lads and to my shame we often had her in tears. She will be with Jesus now but I hope she knows how sorry I am, but more so that I can still remember one lesson that many years later was to change my life, "the parable of the Good Samaritan". In that parable the religious people walked past the man who had been robbed and left for dead, but the hated Samaritan picked him up, put him on his donkey and took him to an inn. He didn't just leave him there, he paid for his keep. Something inside of me that I did not recognise decided I wanted to be like that Samaritan. It seemed like even now we were 'walking past' people who were broken. At that point it put me off religion completely, if I needed putting off, as I had no interest anyway. But now I know that God was preparing me.

One school holiday our housekeeper took me to the Odeon in St Albans to see "*The Inn of the Sixth Happiness.*" It had such an effect on me that we went back to see it again! I did not realise it at the time but God was beginning to prepare me. It was about Gladys Aylward, who as a young woman felt God wanted her to go to China as a missionary. She wrote to the Chinese Mission in London and received a polite reply suggesting she may come for a chat. She packed in her job in Liverpool, moved to London and presented herself at the Mission. They were horrified that she had burnt all her boats and just wanted to go. She had the simple joyful belief that we are all responsible for each other. "But you are not qualified," they said. So she said she would do it without them. She got a job and went to the travel agency to book a train ticket to Wanchim via Tianjin! She saved the money with the travel agent and finally after a very long time the ticket was paid for. She left by train with only a letter of introduction from the Mission in London to the Mission in Wanchim, a small village in China.

When war broke out in that area she walked with hundreds of children over the mountains to the main China Mission and who was there to meet her but the very man who had told her she was not qualified! It is an amazing film.

When I left school I sadly once again drove my dad potty. I had a strange relationship with the local copper who would take me home drunk and tell my dad "I think your son needs to go to bed."

There were times when my life should have ended and yet my Jesus was watching out for me.

My mum used to take my brother Brian and I on holiday to Hastings. On one particular day the weather was bad and the sea was rough, but I insisted on going for a swim. A big wave knocked me down and took me out. Brian noticed and saw me in the wave, fortunately he was able to reach me. My knees were bleeding as the wave had twisted me about but otherwise it was just my pride that was hurt. That very special hand had lifted me up.

On another occasion when I was older I was 'doing a ton' (100mph) on my motorbike along a country lane when I slipped on a bend. How I got out of that with only a hole in my shin bone is a wonder. A miracle! That special hand had been there again.

I am not sure why but at some point I started to go to church with dad and Elaine, my new step-mum, and at the age of eighteen I went forward at a rally. I expected great things the next day but nothing had changed. I continued to go to church, and whenever there was an opportunity I went forward. Looking back there must have been small changes in my life but not the great explosion I had been expecting. I soon became a rebellious teenager again and the relationship with my dad sank to an all-time low. It got so bad that I drew a circle one hundred miles from home and got a job in Wiltshire.

It was then that I got married and Linda my daughter was born in Malmesbury. I then took a job as a machinery rep and our little family moved up to Ilkeston. At that time we were not churchgoers but I did become youth club leader at the local Methodist Church. It was around this time my son Richard was born in Heanor.

Chapter 2

Highfields Farm

I really wanted to own a farm but decided to start up as an Agricultural Contractor – Farm Power Hire instead. That was quite successful and when in 1968 dad bought me a farm, I had all the equipment I needed. (Dad and I had resolved our differences by then.) 'Highfields' was a derelict 100acre farm, the house had been condemned and only eight acres were workable with the rest needing levelling and draining. The price was £23,000! My contracting business was going well, but I made the big mistake of concentrating my efforts on sorting the farm out and lost the income from the business and my dad, bless him, kept bailing me out.

It took thirteen years to restore the house, which had been built in 1752. During this time I made another big mistake of neglecting my wife and family and eventually we split up in 1973. Now I was living in a big house all alone.

I had also become involved in the Queen's Hall Methodist Mission who at that time were raising the money to start a battered wives' home, (now called a Women's Refuge). I said, "I have a big empty house would you like to use it?" They took me up on the offer and so followed my first experience of working with broken people.

In that year I had eighty families through my home. There were black eyes, broken bones all with one thing in common, crying children. At that point in time, I was not what I now know to be a Christian; I was a learner and recognised the value of and need for the love of Jesus. Sad broken people learnt to laugh which began a healing process. I knew how that felt.

I had a lot of help from the Queen's Hall and several ladies came to cook and clean. As leader of the youth club I met Beryl who had become a regular helper.

It was a great day but also a sad day for me when the Queen's Hall purchased a big house outside Derby and all my visitors moved out. All alone again with only my dog for company. It was coming up to Christmas and God reminded me of the bomb site in London and my question to my dad, "Where would Jesus be today daddy?"

I wrote to Social Services and the Police and said, "If you know of anyone with nowhere to go for Christmas send them up to my house."

Well by Christmas Eve the house was full, not a bed to spare and all total strangers, with a fantastic atmosphere.

That evening Beryl, myself and other helpers wrapped dozens of presents donated by local churches and it was gone midnight when they went home, and I collapsed into my bed.

At 3am Christmas morning the phone rang. It was a policeman who had just picked up a man in Derby. He had remembered my letter on the notice board at the station and asked had I still got a bed to spare? The proper answer was no, but I quickly remembered it was Christmas Day and 'that there was no room in the inn' for Jesus. My whole dream of helping others at Christmas and being the 'good Samaritan' would fall apart so I decided to let him have my bed and said "Yes."

Half an hour later there was a knock on the door. There stood a big policeman in a yellow jacket and behind him a filthy bearded man. Without any planning God does amazing things and my horror almost instantly turned to excitement. This will almost certainly be how Jesus will come.

What a privilege! I showed him my bed and I went to sleep on the sofa.

The next day it was all action. Everyone got involved except our new visitor. He would not wake up, it being the first bed he had slept in for a long time.

Lunch was a great experience as were all the chores that followed and then our friend appeared and started picking over the turkey carcass. One of the ladies who had come to help went up to make my bed but soon returned looking ashen. "Roger you must come and see this." My bed was black with lice, thousands of them.

I was in a state of panic having invited all these strangers to my home and I had my first experience of the Salvation Army. I explained the situation on the phone and half an hour later (bless them, it was Christmas Day) a little van and a man in uniform appeared. He rolled up my bed and threw it out of the window telling me to burn it and then remade it with a new mattress, sheets, blankets, and pillows.

By this time (I wish I could remember his name) our visitor was sitting in the lounge. The Salvation Army man took him to the bathroom, bathed him and fitted him out with a new set of clothes.

At this point I need to explain that Beryl and I were engaged and we had invited her mum and dad for tea. To my horror, when I returned to the lounge my future Mother-in-law was sitting in the chair our visitor had recently vacated.

I Want You to Meet My Jesus

Chapter 3

The Day I Learnt to Pray

THAT WAS THE DAY I LEARNT TO PRAY!

"Oh Lord please don't let my future Mother-in-law get lice." I had been brought up to see prayer as a religious experience with recognised jargon, even maybe a prayer written a hundred years ago as the 'prayer for today'. Yet I have come to know that God wants to hear how you feel and what your need is. Believe me I was desperate, and He certainly heard that prayer as none of our visitors including mum were affected. It was some months later on our wedding day and too late to change her mind that mum was told.

After Christmas once again I was on my own and somehow got involved with homeless youngsters. Most of these had a criminal record and so it was that I got involved with the Youth Offending Service (YOS) and that was my life for a while. There is a gap in my memory but Beryl and I got more involved with the Etwall Methodists and more importantly Youth for Christ (YFC). We also had a growing feeling that God was calling us, that He wanted us and the farm as a refuge, an ARK. I have always hated jargon but I cannot put it into words how we knew that. A mixture of verses from the Bible, a sermon at church that spoke to us or just a comment from a friend; probably all of those things. Believe me if you want to meet my Jesus He will respond. But first you need to be willing.

Beryl got on really well with my children Linda and Richard and after we got married in 1978 there is quite a gap. I believe that God has a plan for everyone. The beginning of that plan is preparation. The Bible says that He knows us even in our mother's womb. This gap was allowing our little family to grow and to prepare us for the future. Nicky was born in 1980 and Kelly came along in 1983.

When Nicky was just five months old Richard was run over by a one-ton roller pulled by a tractor. How he was not killed on the spot was a miracle on its own. There he lay screaming in pain and his arm bone stuck up through his jacket. An ambulance rushed him to hospital where they plastered his arm and sent him home telling me to get him walking as his legs were bruised and needed exercising.

The next day his stomach was blue and distended and he was in great pain, so I took him back to hospital and an x-ray showed that his pelvis was cracked both sides. He also had internal injuries and bleeding that required four pints of blood by transfusion.

The accident happened on a Bank Holiday Monday and on Wednesday we were told that he would have to lie on his back for a month and then learn to walk again. By the Saturday he was in such terrible pain, and as I sat by his bedside in hospital, I felt so helpless that I asked him if he would like me to pray for him. To my astonishment he said "yes" so it must have hurt a lot! I laid my hands on his tummy and just asked God to make him better. When I got home I was in a real state, sure that he was close to death, and so I wrote a letter to our steward at our church to ask the congregation to pray for Richard that Sunday.

Eight days later he walked out of that hospital, two weeks to the day since the accident and there wasn't a mark on his x-ray. I cannot understand why, but I was so shocked I didn't go to church for six months. I didn't really understand at the time what had happened and only later did I thank God giving Him the glory.

It was at this time we were having a lot of trouble with our neighbour further down the drive. It seemed that however hard we tried not to cause him any bother, something happened to upset him, and it did become a real problem to us. Everything got so out of proportion that we decided that God was telling us to move. Our daily Bible readings seemed to lead us to that conclusion, so we very begrudgingly set out to find the house that God wanted for us.

Each time we went to see somewhere new we always felt the same when we got home, 'Highfields is the house we want'. Still all the problems persisted and so we kept looking. This went on for some time, and truthfully I cannot remember what changed our attitude, but suddenly we were not fighting any longer.

We really wanted what God wanted for us and if that meant moving then we were ready. Immediately things changed and God quite clearly told us that He wanted us to stay at Highfields and that He wanted to use us there. In fact, all He had been waiting for was for us to be prepared to live wherever He put us. So we followed what He wanted and not what we wanted.

If only we can trust Him that His plan for us is perfect, then we can release all of our desires and ambitions into His keeping. He may well use our ambition for He knows all that we desire, but if His plans move away from or alter those ambitions then we should be able to trust Him, as His ways are not our ways and our ways not His ways. God had taught us a powerful lesson but at that time we still did not really 'know' Him.

I Want You to Meet My Jesus

Chapter 4

A New Beginning

We were told of a couple in Derby who had an amazing counselling ministry. They were too busy to come and see us and we were advised to make an appointment to see them. However, on the following evening, we were told that a friend had decided to phone them on our behalf only to be told that God had told them of a couple with a farm and how He wanted to use it. They came out to us the very next day and then began the most painful part of our search. They pointed out areas of our life that were not right, areas in which the devil had a real hold, and they began to tell us about the existence of the third person, 'the Holy Spirit'.

There followed many weeks of soul searching and prayer. We tried several times to meet this couple again, but something always got in the way until we realised the devil was stopping us, so come what may we decided one day to go. Almost immediately the weather changed, and it was perfect for planting thousands of brussels sprout plants that were long overdue. We prayed and asked God into the situation. Sure enough next day 'out of the blue' a friend arrived at the farm and asked if we needed any help, so the sprouts got planted and we were able to go. We had learnt yet another lesson.

That day we learnt more of this Jesus and the Holy Spirit and we now wanted to 'be filled'. I asked how this could happen and was given a little book entitled 'The Way Ahead'. I was really keen. It said to read the first half and then if that was what I wanted to read the second half and ask the Spirit to fill me. "Don't go to bed till you have received" it continued. Well, I prayed my heart out until 3am. I was feeling worse instead of better and went to bed shattered. I should add that Beryl had a much more simple approach to things. I expected to feel different in the morning. Morning came and it could not have been worse. Everything went wrong. I could not find anything and everything I touched seemed to break. Needless to say I got cross with God and wondered where I had gone wrong.

Some days later I related this sad story to our friends and the reaction was not quite what I expected "Praise the Lord you really got the devil worried. He thought he was losing you," they said.

When we pray we need to pray with faith. I could have gone to bed straight away if I had trusted Him. I should have praised the Lord regardless the next day and after each problem. Yet another important lesson learned. The devil will let us carry on with our way of life while it suits him. When the battle starts he will try to prove God is a liar, because with the things of God we have to exercise our faith, with the things of the devil we can see and feel them and they bring short term, if any, pleasure.

At the next YFC Sunday rally Beryl went forward for healing from her hay fever. I prayed hard for her and looked up to see her stretched out on the floor. She had been 'slain in the Spirit'. I didn't know what that was at the time, but the Lord certainly did a good job on her. Her hay fever was cured and as an extra gift she had a new prayer language and was full of excitement over it all.

As for me, I asked to receive and on the same evening two friends laid hands on me. They kept praying but nothing happened. Then I remembered to believe and receive. I began to feel warm all over and my back which had been damaged when I was a teenager was healed. Sure enough the next day we were tested and we were ready, full of faith and our search was over! Or so we thought.

Four days later we were praying with some friends in the lounge at the farm and I was suddenly overcome with a deep sadness and started to cry. Tears rolled down my cheeks and I knew I had just lost a dear friend. "Who could it be?" I thought and then I realised it was me, The old Roger, who had just died, so that the new Roger who God had promised me was alive. I had been born again.

We didn't go to bed that night till 3am. We were just drunk with excitement, singing, and praising the Lord and gabbling away. Oh, the search seemed to have been forever but the prize was worth every minute of it.

Some months before we were born again there was a checklist in our *'Every Day with Jesus'* notes. It was really a personal look at our lives to see if we were following the principles that the Bible lays down and that we were using our time and money wisely. To our horror we only got four out of ten! We vowed to improve the situation, copied that list out and re-read it regularly. Unfortunately however hard we tried there was little change and as with all good ideas that prove difficult our enthusiasm waned and we lost the list.

Sometime after we were born again we found the list again and re-checked it. To our amazement changes had happened within us that in our own strength we had failed to make and we had not even noticed. God had once again kept His promise to us. So whatever state your life is in take heart do not wait until you have changed for that may never happen. Trust your Jesus now.

Happiness

I wonder have you ever tried
To see life from the other side.
As God would see us from above
To see how we abuse His love.

The greater things like war and strife
That desecrate, destroy our life,
The needless suffering we cause
To satisfy our basic flaws.

The smaller things like tiffs at home
The rudeness, spite, and those alone
The way we hurt the ones we love
Without a thought for Him above.

If we could love as He would do
See with eyes He sees us through
Then life for all would be divine
From now until the end of time.

I Want You to Meet My Jesus

Chapter 5

Foster Parents

At that time Beryl's mum showed us an advert in the Derby Telegraph for a young girl looking for a foster home on a farm. We applied and were accepted. We had to go to classes and one thing we were told was to look for and encourage anything that was good.

Jane had been in care since she was six months old in various foster homes. She was now thirteen years old, very mixed up and was difficult to live with. She knew how to push all the wrong buttons. She started going to the local school with some success but at home she was awful. She also ended up in hospital after trying to hurt herself.

I am not one for getting angry but one time we were having a big argument, and stormed out of the lounge, slamming the door so hard it broke a hinge. I went down the field, sat under an oak tree, and cried "Lord get her out of our home." There was no answer. "Lord this is really bad for our children, get her out of our home." "*Ask me for a new love for her.*" "No way! Just get her out of our home." This went on for quite a while, (you will discover God has a lot of patience) until I said, "OK Lord but you will have to give me a new love for her." I went back into the house and found her still sitting on the floor where I had left her. I could not stop myself; I just threw my arms around her and we both cried. That is my Jesus and if you ask Him, He will give you a love for the unlovable.

Love

Oh Lord your beauty rises high
In mud and rock and trees
And all the clouds that fly the skies
And all the birds and bees.

Love is born in all these things
And cherished by us all
Your love for us has dove-like wings
To catch us lest we fall.

Our love for fellow man is weak
Compared with Your love for us.
Our shame is deep, our hearts are meek
And we ask you to forgive us.

So lead us, Father, show the way
For us to cure the ills of man

And take us forward to the day
When the whole world says, "We can".

15th January 2021 -

Another Covid19 lockdown.

Forgive me but I must stop for a few days – it is January 2021, we are locked down, over 1,000 people will die today and I am still struggling at losing the farm despite knowing it had to go (more about that later.) Despite my faith I am struggling to write this. I am wading through heaps of notes from thirty years ago and getting quite emotional or to put it bluntly I am not handling it very well. The good news is Father knows. He will comfort me and I will be back again.

Although embarrassing I feel it important to re-live my down days of which there have been many and have been on anti-depressants several times. Then you have a choice, you can ditch the whole idea of becoming a Christian, but even if you do Jesus' hand is still reaching out to you, or you can get down on your knees and cry out "Lord I can't manage without you."

It has rained heavily during the night but I decided to go for a walk and a pray. There is water everywhere and I am so pleased I am no longer a farmer. I still get broody and with lockdown and being used to working with a lot of young people I am really lost and lonely. Beryl did offer to come with me, but I needed to be on my own and pray. It's ironic that after years of working and longing to have time together we are now locked down together. We almost see too much of each other!"

Chapter 6

The Barn

You will remember that Beryl and I met whilst I was running a women's refuge. Naturally when we married it was necessary for us to start our own home, but as our children arrived we realised that the experience of helping the battered wives and the probation youngsters had stirred something within us and that was that we wanted to do again. Our house was really only big enough for our family but sixteen feet away from the house stood an old barn. Some of the timbers we were told came out of a boat in the 1500's and it was in a very bad state of repair. The date on the wall of the barn was 1742; the house had a later date on its wall – 1752.

We could both see that the barn could be used to accommodate people in need, and so very soon after we married we started to pray that God would use the barn. As the years rolled by we watched the roof and the first floor cave in and we became quite impatient as the barn fell more and more into disrepair.

There was also beginning to be a lot of talk in the village about *"them dropouts at the farm"* so we decided to do a bit of PR. We sent out our first newsletter. I think there were about fifty at the time. Beryl and I felt it was about time we put out a shortened version of *"What's happening at Highfields."*

It is really a story that was started by an overwhelming urge to work with broken people with all we have. This in turn led to many areas of our lives that we still kept to ourselves, and God could not use them in His way. This process is still happening, and I guess will continue to happen for the rest of our lives.

At that time we learnt a lot in a variety of ways, spiritual and practical. We came to understand that all the young people who came to us were angry. They had every reason to be angry and they needed a safe place to be angry, and often someone to vent their anger on (once resulting in me with a broken collar bone). On another occasion it was so bad that I screamed at the lad that he would have to go. I felt like God hit me in the face with a brick. *"That is the way that lad has been talked to all his life."*

I went into the house, found Beryl, told her what had happened and we sat and prayed. On that day we made the decision that we would never ask anyone to leave. Being angry was a key part of their healing and they needed a place to do that.

Another lesson we learnt was that God knew every detail of our needs; He would never leave us or forsake us and one of those needs for us was time out. At that time there was a lot of 'time-shares' about and we seemed to be on a mailing list for free weekend offers.

One in particular was to Lakelands in Ambleside in the Lake District. The only condition of these offers was that we spent an hour with a rep. We accepted the offer and duly went to the office for our sales chat. Being a good salesman he started the interview by asking what we do for a living, so we told him all about Highfields. He was so enthralled that we took up most of the hour and he said, "Don't bother buying an apartment, just let me know when you can come." Wow! We had a free holiday for a few years after that up until the time he left. Even after that time was up we continued to go and still do as it is a very special place for us.

Here I have included a few events that led us to be sure that God was now ready to use the farm.

January 1984 - We were introduced to a couple who had a vision for a couple with a farm and God wanted to use it.

June 1984 - At a YFC meeting at the farm a stranger had a vision of the fields covered in white and people coming from many places to find God. The white he felt were tents. Another at the same meeting had a prophecy concerning a school for evangelism. (Thirty five years later that would describe Betel. God's got a lot of patience.)

November 1984 - Both Beryl and I independently but on the same evening had a clear vision of the old barn, not with a sixteen-foot gap but joined to our house. God was waiting for our commitment that the barn should be PART of our home. We both drew sketches of what we had seen and they were identical. We prayed that evening that the Lord would send us someone who could draw the plans for us to confirm the vision and the very next day we were introduced to Oliver Eley who agreed to handle the planning side of things.

Have you ever read a book and then phoned the author? Someone gave me a well-worn copy of "Miracle Valley" by Jim Wilkinson. It's a great story of Hollybush Farm and of Jim and Cynthia's tussle with the Holy Spirit. Prior to buying Hollybush they had a pig farm in a local village in Yorkshire. Their pigs got swine fever twice resulting both times in all their pigs being slaughtered. While I was reading the book we were preparing for lambing. Our ewes were really healthy and then disaster struck, they got twin lamb disease just before giving birth and we lost half the flock. Needless to say, we prayed like mad.

In the back of his book was Jim Wilkinson's name, address, and telephone number. Little did I know it then but Jim was to become our spiritual father and later on I of course realised that if those sheep had not died, I would never have contacted him.

In May 1985 we went to the Hollybush Youth Camp 'Miracle Valley' with our daughters and the youngsters who were living with us. We had an amazing time. It was almost as if God were showing us what could happen at Highfields. When we got home there was a pink envelop on the doorstep with £15 inside. Three days before planning permission was granted we had the £15 towards the project from a stranger and in this the Lord confirmed that He would provide all we would need, and that His timing is always perfect.

Two days before planning permission was granted a stranger approached us at a meeting in Kegworth where Beryl and I had been singing. He asked us to let him know when we had the planning permission for the barn as he would like to build it for us, as long as we provided the materials. He was from the Youth Training Service (YTS). Planning permission was then granted and money had started to come in. Our God is so good if we trust him in all things and His timing is perfect.

Chapter 7

CARE

All along we did not know how God was going to use the barn, and so we got in touch with CARE (Christian Action Research Education) who were looking for 1,000 Christian homes that would be prepared to take in teenage mums and other young people in severe need. These vulnerable people required a good base in which to feel at home in their time of need and help with finding accommodation.

CARE was looking for a regional co-ordinator and I applied for the job. We were invited to London for an interview with Dr Ann Townsend the then director. At the end of the interview she asked her secretary to take us out for lunch. After lunch she took us back into her office – she explained that she really wanted to give us the job but felt God was telling her not to hence sending us out for lunch so she could pray. She told us she felt God was saying that we should concentrate on the vision He had given us.

So much happened in 1984/5. That was when Billy Graham was running Crusades up and down the country and we got involved with 'Mission Sheffield'.

In 1984 our village decided to organise two buses to go to Villa Park in Birmingham. I half-heartedly asked a few people to come, I even helped to deliver a few leaflets around the village but needless to say no-one came as a result of my encouragement. A salesman who really believes in his product will succeed, one who is doubtful fails: In fact, no-one went forward from those two buses.

Etwall was not yet ready to receive a group of new believers, but God had a different purpose for that trip and used it in a wonderful way. The week after Villa Park those of us who went met together afterwards to discuss our feelings. It turned out to be such a brilliant evening of praise and sharing and the Etwall Christian Fellowship (ECF) was born.

There were Methodists, Baptists, and Anglicans all meeting together in fellowship. This was for most of us the first time we had seriously met together outside our own church group and for me a milestone in my journey with Jesus – He never called us to be Methodists or anything else just Happy Christians.

A Thought on Christian Unity

A nurse asked me what Faith I was
I said, "A Christian, will that do?"
She said, "What sort I need to know."
I thought awhile and told her true
"There are only two sorts, good or bad
I try my best but fear I'm bad"

She could not put that on her form
Only Methodist, C of E or other norm
But what is all the fuss about?
My Saviour is the same for all
No matter what you call yourself
The same Dear Jesus comforts when we
call.

So let's forget this us and them
And shut our eyes and count to ten.
Pray a while and open them
And see the world that Jesus gave us
And let him come
And let Him save us.

Most of my writing at this time reveals a pressure
both of the size of the project and from various
discouragements that we had been receiving
from people. We had some wonderful friends
and prayer partners and these people helped us
to see that the barn and all of the other problems
are God's and not ours: We really can snuggle up
in His arms and await His guidance and blessings

otherwise we will burn out with worry and be unable to listen. Will I ever learn?

Discouragement is perhaps the most difficult thing to deal with because you can easily begin to believe that the discourager is right. My diary has been a great blessing to me because I can check back and read how we come to be doing what we are doing from God's guidance to me, or as I was once told "go back to where my axe was sharp".

We were becoming desperate. The money was getting low, and it seemed that everyone had lost interest on the financial front. I was longing to share it with the fellowship but that just seemed as if we were asking for money, so once again we took the problem to the Lord and asked Him to deal with it in His own wonderful way, and oh boy how He lifted us up!

I love to think of the wonderful Christmas story and I wonder about the inn keeper who said "there was no room at the inn" for Mary and Joseph and was only able to offer them a dusty stable.

We are all inn keepers of today. Is there a room in your hearts for the young people who are feeling so hurt and unloved today? It is not a government problem, no it is the church's problem. It's all of ours: Jesus was born and died to show us how to love. Anything short of that and we become the inn keeper who had no room.

Excerpt from one of our prayer letters

"It is a year now since we sent out our first prayer letter and to those who have prayed with us and for us, we say thank you. Mountains have been moved, our lives have been transformed and all that has happened to the old barn is becoming an example for others to follow. Actually our faith in the vision has been tested again and again but we have kept our eyes on that vision.

A lot of work has been done to prepare the barn for its new roof and it is our aim to have it watertight in time for Christmas. Prayers have been wonderfully answered and it would be impossible to list them all without describing the circumstances in which they occurred. Beryl and I would like to share some of those experiences; we are not qualified preachers, but we are on fire for Jesus and have dedicated our lives to this work."

Immediately after sending a second prayer letter out a Christian builder friend told us he was finishing a job and would help us with the roof in December!

At this point two Bible passages encouraged us

"As long as Moses held up his hands the Israelites were winning, but when he lowered his hands the Amalekites were winning. Aaron and Hur held his hands up, one on one side and one on the other."
Exodus 17:11-12 (NIV)

"And this is my prayer that your love may abound more and more in depth and insight."
Philippians 1:9 (NIV)

What a wonderful book the Bible is when you get to know the One who wrote it.

I am so grateful to Brenda Cotton who encouraged me to write things down as I would never have remembered the scriptures and the prayer which formed such a foundation to our early search for Jesus, and how nothing will happen without prayer and the Bible.

When I pray coincidences happen and when I don't they don't!

During the early part of the winter of 1985 it seemed that nothing was happening and so I spent a lot of time on my own, sharing my problems with God and learning to listen to His voice. I had a job convincing myself that I was not being lazy, but that period played a very important part in helping me to see things clearly and know the way ahead.

2021 - I have to write this bit with sadness – I am copying these notes from years ago. It was all so new and fresh but now I seem to have lost that faith and need to go back to 'where my axe was sharp'. It is also too easy to think that everything is going wrong – or not happening – when in fact God is busy. I need to remember that my ways are not His ways and His ways are not my ways!

God can use our weaknesses and writing has always been one of mine. All of the notes used for this book have been hand written, and I have also had to write many letters to businesses over the years with such a great response. I haven't just written willy-nilly but have responded to a nudge that I cannot explain. There is a wonderful 'feeling' when God is prompting you and He promises to make us strong in our broken places. When we are weak we are strong in Him.

I Want You to Meet My Jesus

Chapter 8

The God of Restoration

At this time we had a visit from a reporter from the Burton Daily Mail who gave us a wonderful write-up. We also got a plug on Radio Derby. In both cases prayer was wonderfully answered, and the local media started reporting on us regularly, followed by the TV. I have a file of hundreds of news cuttings and DVDs from this period.

At this time, my diary shows days of emptiness and despair and yet a growing realisation that all the necessities of life are not so necessary and that God really is aware of all our needs and will provide, so my faith was gently growing.

And yet – how can my days be full of emptiness and despair when so many amazing things were happening? Simply because I did not recognise the hand of God.

Apart from materials, our first practical need was scaffolding for the main barn. I must have thought that the tiles would have got up on that roof all on their own. We could have hired scaffolding but that would have been expensive for the amount we needed and the length of time it would have taken, so again we put it to the Lord. Within twenty four hours we had been loaned three scaffolding towers and enough scaffolding and boards to do most of the way round. (There was a twelve foot gap).

We were hoping to start re-roofing the next morning. Again we prayed, and that same day we met a gentleman who works for a local building firm. They had a tower that was not in use which I could fetch that day and you guessed it! It fitted the gap exactly as if it had been made to fit.

On 2nd December work was to start on the roof tiles. The great day had arrived and what did it do? It rained. Not the best weather for working on a roof, so Phil, Beryl and I sat round the kitchen table and prayed and praised God. At 10.30am there was a knock on the door and there stood a rep from a local builders' merchants. He was interested in the barn and even more interested to hear that God was involved. In fact, all the management of his company were Christians, and not only did he agree to let us have an account with them but we ordered £500-worth of materials that arrived in our yard that afternoon.

We made a good start the next day when a car pulled into the yard. I heard a voice,"Mr. Hosking?" "Yes that's me." "I was given one of your prayer letters a year ago and I thought I would come and see you. We have prayed for you every day since." Wasn't that wonderful! After a year of prayer he came on the day we started. Also, to round off the week we were given £600 which paid for the roofing materials.

When all the practical work started it was difficult to stop and listen to the Lord and to continue with Bible study and prayer. But it had become such a part of my life now that I knew it had become the 'most important part'. We had already seen that with God's help the practical side just flies along.

We were watertight by 21st December and so we had a lovely little service. I have included some photos, one of which is Kelly, at two years old in a white sheet, with wings, and a runny nose, stood in the last remaining manger. We borrowed a donkey from a neighbour. We put out bales for fifty people and fifty people turned up.

One couple, who came were Jan, and Geoff, with five children, who have faithfully turned up for our monthly prayer meetings right up to the last one in November 2020.

It was a very meaningful experience with all the cobwebs and dust and straw and little children acting the scene. We decided not to have an offering however we still received one hundred and fifty pounds.

On Christmas Day we had another miracle, unrelated to the barn and yet demonstrating to us as a family how God was becoming a very real, accessible, and caring Father in our home.

Beryl's mum and dad were coming for lunch. The turkey weighing sixteen pounds and stuffed at both ends was put into the oven on Christmas Eve with the automatic timer set for 5.30am the following morning. At 9am we came downstairs only to find the oven had not come on. Beryl then proceeded to have a nervous breakdown as it appeared Christmas dinner was to be a very late event and with such important visitors too! We sat down, calmed down and either had to accept things and have lunch at 4pm or we could pray about it. Praise God we decided to do the latter and I found myself praying that our oven would be turned into a microwave. We were so confident that we switched the oven on at 9.30am and proceeded with all the other preparations. At 11am Beryl rather gingerly had a peep and to our utter amazement it was completely cooked, and we ended up having lunch half an hour early. All of us including our extended family witnessed this amazing miracle!

The basic crumbling barn pictured a year ago (right) has been completely remoulded and modernised into a smart new building (above).

The original barn photo taken in 1984 (right photo) and 6 years later in 1990 (above)

As it is today (2022)

Lifting the old beams out of the second barn (1990)

As it is today (2022)

**Christmas 1985
in the old barn.**

The roof is on!!

In the new year Butterley Brick phoned and offered to give us all the bricks we needed to build the extension to join the barn to the house, and the next day we had a call from Teen Challenge at Stoke on Trent who were a group also involved in reaching out with the Gospel to young people. They were offering to help us two of whom were professional plasterers. More miracles from the God who created this beautiful world.

Shortly after this we heard from Dulux who wanted to give us all the paint we needed. They advised if we could have the barn painted by 14th August it would be entered into a national community project competition in the September. We won the competition and received £500! Two of the lads came to London with me to receive the cheque.

Some really dreadful things happened to us too at different times, and you had to wonder how God allowed them to happen. But we are always dealing with other human beings like ourselves who are on their own journey.

A Trust came into our lives and the couple leading it joined our prayer group. Their vision had been to provide holiday accommodation for young people, but it had not got anywhere for some time and our vision for Highfields seemed to fit theirs. So their trustees decided to close the trust and to transfer the money to us. We didn't hear from them for some time but were really excited that a considerable amount of money was on its way.

Then one evening they came to us in a bad state. They sat at the kitchen table and cried. They had cashed in the money from the trust and spent it. They had clearly broken the law and we never did find out what happened, but we were to learn the lesson of forgiveness which I really struggled with. Even years later it kept cropping up in my mind. God had wanted to provide. They were a lovely couple and we had felt so sorry for them but the implication for the barn was that work had to slow down and stop.

As a group we went out carol singing "Nothing strange about that" you may say – but there was a difference. We prayed before we set off and carried a Bible with us, reading it at different points around the village. We hadn't gone out to sing a few seasonal songs and collect money to prop up our church, we went out with Jesus, for Jesus, and we refused money that was offered (politely of course) much to the surprise of those who offered it.

At Easter time 1985 we followed a similar pattern and carried a cross with us with the same purpose in mind. Our village was witnessing a changing mood, a determination by a few ordinary folk to tell everyone about the saving grace of Jesus.

And then Mission Sheffield – yes you have guessed – two buses but this time there were twelve new believers.

Also in 1985 we held several youth camps in a marquee. I remember on one occasion the weather was so bad that they pitched the tents inside the marquee.

At that time, our prayer meetings were still happening, and my sister received a letter from a friend:

"We were praying about the picture you shared the other night and we feel God gave an interpretation. We felt the boundaries of the farm were as the hedges mentioned in Job, God hedging in His people for protection. We believe you were right about the presence of the Holy Spirit on the farm but you mentioned a darkness that could obviously not be the Lord. We feel there is an oppression over the farm – there are dark forces pressing down – there is life, air, the Spirit under the darkness but it is quickly being expended like being in an airless room. You only have a certain amount of oxygen before it runs out.

The Lord is waiting to pour His life-giving Spirit into the farm – the rustling wind – but there isn't a hole in the darkness, and the Spirit can't get through until a breach is made in the darkness through praise and spiritual warfare."

We were learning to hear from God in so many different ways and needless to say we took this very seriously.

There was a unanimous feeling concerning our ministry that we were being called to love. One small word which sounded so simple. But over the years we have hurt so much inside as we have shared people's pain. This was also wise advice as we have witnessed over the years that some people feel they have to do everything. There are specialist ministries, particularly counselling, where terrible damage can be done. When we are befriending someone, it is important to recognise the time to stop and ask for help.

Money started to come in for the barn and a small group of lads helped me to strip off the old tiles ready for the new roof on the second part of the barn.

I Want You to Meet My Jesus

Chapter 9

Heart Searching

At this stage I must relate a part of our private life that at the time caused us a lot of pain and heart searching, but it also finally put us in a position of starting to trust in the Lord.

In 1981 the farm was one hundred and thirty two acres – one hundred owned by my dad and thirty two owned by us. We had a huge overdraft and were getting a bit fed up with just working to pay the interest at around 15%. So we sold eighty acres to a neighbour. My dad very generously just took the money the land had cost him with the balance to pay off the overdraft. The next year I sold a further twenty acres in order to start a small second-hand car business with a friend in Derby.

The business grew well but my partner was experiencing personal problems and decided to pull out. This left me with the decision to either let the business go and lose quite a lot of money or try to run it myself. If I could get the garage big enough I could bring in a manager, and then the business would keep myself and my family financially whilst we looked after the occupants of the barn.

To begin with my efforts as a second-hand car salesman went really well. I began to realise that it does not pay to be too honest when selling cars and success and pride began to take a hand. The vision for the farm became less important to me. The car industry at that time was struggling due to the new 'C' plate coming in and the main dealers were offering huge discounts on new cars. Our sales stopped almost overnight.

Our pastor's car kept breaking down so I decided to give him one of my cars. Dad then sent me a news cutting about the 'Missionary Aviation Fellowship'. They needed an estate car and so again I decided to give them one. This sounds dreadful now as I write from notes thirty-six years ago, but I felt sure that God would bless me and my business. Well you can't bribe God and we went spectacularly bust. God said to me *"They were my cars and I did not tell you to give them away!"*

This was a lesson that has stayed with me over the years. If you give something over to God, He has the right to tell you when to release it. We ended up having to arrange an auction sale.

At this stage we learnt another very important lesson too. We had for some time been surrounded by some very loving, caring Christian friends. We should always listen to advice, but we should ACT only on what we feel sure God is telling us. As the day of the sale drew near a very much respected and dear friend said we should trust God to sell all the items for their true value and not put a reserve on them. In my heart I knew God was telling me to accept whatever happened at the sale, but I wanted to believe the advice I had been given. So I removed all the reserves for all but the best cars.

The sale should have realised £40,000 but actually realised £9,000 with some cars left unsold. That is called double minded, and I was certainly learning the hard way. I have always been a proud capable person and the potter can only work the clay if the clay is soft and pliable. I do not blame God in any way because I could see that I was the problem. I was not giving Him authority over all things and could not accept that He was capable of providing for all our needs.

During the time we were running the Estate Car Centre, we were baptised at Willington Baptist Church by Jim Wilkinson of Hollybush, after which I was sitting in the office when I felt that God gave me a scripture, "*For I know the plans I have for you declares the Lord. Plans to prosper you and not to harm you, plans to give you hope and a future. Then you will call on me and come and pray to me and I will listen to you; you will seek me and find me when you seek me with all your heart."* Jeremiah 29:11-14 (NIV). This seemed like a great tender hand that was reaching out to me, like a father who sheds tears when his son hurts himself.

Several people had started to pray with us about the cars that remained. I spent a lot of money on adverts but they started to sell in ways that could only be an answer to prayer, so we stopped advertising and started trusting.

When we first had planning permission for the barn it was prophesied that God would not need our money, and that He would provide. I had not accepted that and had tried to earn it, but then we were in a position of having planning permission, with no job and no money!

Looking back on it now it would not have been much glory to God if the Estate Car Centre paid all the bills. All that happened since that day has proved to us that the God of the Bible is still the God of today.

At that time people were telling me to get a job. I had responsibilities and yet I felt sure that God wanted me to focus on the restoration of the barn and to look after young people with big problems. I knew this could not be done in my spare time. We just had to trust in the God that was calling us and believe in His promises to provide as He does for the lilies of the field.

On 1st November Elaine gave Beryl a cheque for the housekeeping. It was still in the kitchen in May when we had to use it before it became out of date. I should add that the housekeeping was a lot of money as we had up to four young people staying with us at that time and many helpers working on the barn. There were often fifteen people sitting round the table and on one day we served forty two meals. It reminds me of the parable of the loaves and fishes.

Enough and More

As we sit down to eat our lunch
Prepared by our dear mum,
We realise that half the world
Have got an empty tum.

The food we eat and take for granted
Many would feel spoiled.
If half that much was given us
Roasted fried or boiled.

This world it is a crazy place
Too much where others are short,
And yet with selfish man in charge
"What more can you expect", I thought.

And yet if we left God in charge
To lead us day by day,
Then there would be enough to eat
And spare to give away.

January 2021 - This lockdown seems worse than the last one. Then we could sunbathe and just enjoy doing nothing. Not this time though. It snowed really heavy yesterday and I am struggling to fill my days. This sounds bad but I cannot be bothered to do anything, I have lost my motivation. Beryl is having a wonderful time sewing, baking, and now home-schooling Tayla. I feel quite jealous, which I know doesn't make sense. I am really struggling with this book which also doesn't make sense either as God is really shouting at me to carry on. On Saturday Ian came to the door and said, "Have you started that book yet? Can't wait to read it."

This morning I was up at Betel. One of the guys asked me how I was, and I tried to explain how I had no motivation, that I was trying to write a book about this place (Betel). "Oh," he said, "you must let me put my testimony at the end. I would have been dead if it hadn't been for Betel." God is doing His best to motivate me, so I came home and I am typing again. Then the phone rings and Mel, who has been part of our extended family for the past thirty years, is on the phone. She asked me what I was doing and I told her. "Oh, I can't wait to read that." She replies.

What I am trying to say is that God is making it very clear what He wants me to do, and I am being very stubborn and I can't understand why. Perhaps I do not want to re-live some parts of my story.

A lot of what I am writing is copied from notes made from that time and it's amazing the detail I have. I am now reminded of the story of Jonah. He knew what God was telling him to do but he used any excuse not to be obedient and it was the fish carrying him to where he needed to be that changed his mind!. I do hope that a big fish doesn't swallow me.

"Please God I know what you are telling me to do, please motivate me." *"I am trying, Rog, but you are not listening."*

I Want You to Meet My Jesus

Chapter 10

Our Walk to the Lake

Some years ago some friends and I drove to Wales to find somewhere to camp. After driving down many dead-end lanes and up many more mountain tracks totally unsuitable for a car with three adults and six children on board, we finally came across a lake just off the A5 past Betws-y-Coed.

When Beryl and I got married I took her to this lovely place. In fact it played a very important part of her getting to know my children Linda and Richard and we became regular visitors to the place up until our first baby, Nicky was born. We did try once with her as a baby and enjoyed it but with the arrival of, Kelly, our youngest child we started to spend our holidays in rented cottages where the facilities were more suitable for a young family.

During the early part of 1986 we were getting to know our foster daughter Jane as well as desiring to tell all the lads that worked with us about our Jesus.

We were getting more young people joining us on the farm but somehow everything seemed to take a sudden negative turn.

Our days were so busy, and our morning quiet times became smaller or not at all, so we hit with the idea of sharing it after breakfast with the lads that came to the farm. I believe that was a near fatal error as we were then putting ourselves into a giving situation instead of receiving one and if we cease to receive then we cease to have anything to give.

During a particular week in July 1986 everything seemed to be against us. The lads were getting unruly - two had spent the day picking on another lad who had mental disabilities and who enjoyed coming to the farm for some peace. They wanted to know where he had left his 'handbag' and similar remarks meant to destroy and hurt. I was really cut up when I heard about it that evening, as one of those responsible had many problems of his own and the other, believe it or not, went forward at Mission Sheffield only two weeks previously.

To cap it all Jane our foster daughter was really testing our love for her. It seemed that as she felt more secure in our home, she felt more able to tip me out like the cuckoo in the nest. We had been told that her father and other men who shared a home with her and her mum had been a constant failure to her, and she was afraid that I would let her down. And so the pressure built up. Where were we going wrong? We didn't even have time to spend with the Lord each morning or if we were honest even the inclination. That of course was the punch line; once the devil gets his mucky paws into our lives, all he wants to do is destroy and cause unhappiness and spiritual death.

We decided we desperately needed a break from it all and so we started to pray in earnest. They say that the churches are always full when there is a war on. We can always find time to pray when we are desperate! How we must hurt God with our selfishness. Still His Love for us is perfect; He hears and listens and very often answers at these times to show how complete His Love is for us.

Linda's boyfriend had offered to look after Kelly, Nicky, and Jane for us on the coming Friday and so the family could look after themselves for a long weekend.

On the Friday morning Jim Wilkinson from Hollybush phoned us at 7.30am, as the Lord had laid us on his heart at that time - what a confirmation for the weekend!

We entrusted ourselves, the family and home we were leaving behind to the Lord and set off complete with tent etc. to our favourite camping spot in Wales.

As we were leaving the farm the sky was black and the rain was coming down in torrents. The weather forecast for the weekend country wide was bad as several friends had taken great pains to tell us, but as we sat in the car ready to leave we just asked the Lord to keep us dry. As we drove out of the yard there were two doves sitting on the gate and our hearts felt at peace for the first time in what seemed like ages.

It rained on and off all the way there and we sent up an extra prayer (oh ye of little faith). As we drove through Betws-y-Coed sure enough the sky was blue over our field until we got the tent up then down it came again, but we were in the dry with all our things.

Come Saturday morning after a good lie in we awoke to find the tent full of flies. We had forgotten to bring any fly spray. We did our reading from our 'Every Day with Jesus' booklet and had a good prayer time but still the things pestered us. Things like that drive Beryl potty and they were obviously going to cause us to fall out until we realised the devil was out to spoil our day with some success. We prayed in the name of Jesus that they would leave us alone and from that moment on until we went out of the tent not one fly landed on either of us.

We so often restrict God to big things and big plans, but He wants us to be happy, and just like our earthly fathers just loves to be asked to help us with our little problems *"Do not be anxious about anything, but in every situation, by prayer and petition, with thanksgiving, present your requests to God. And the peace of God, which transcends all understanding, will guard your hearts and your minds in Christ Jesus."* Philippians 4:6 (NIV).

At this point we had another problem. We had come away for some peace, and as we left home we decided we must share it with God. On Saturday we had the choice of going shopping (did I really write that!!) which we could do at home or go for a walk in the hills. We felt so tired that that didn't really appeal to us. We wanted to return to the lake but there was a very long uphill mountain climb to reach it. This is where we thought we should go but the thought of the climb just bent our minds, so we decided to try a different approach. We didn't have a map of the area but I knew the general direction, so we packed a bag with a drink and some crisps and of course (oh ye of little faith again) our raincoats and set off. Would you believe it that in forty-five minutes we were at the lake side. In fact we were there so soon that we didn't feel like a break and were ready for more. The Lord really spoke to us through that experience.

How we look at the challenge that the Bible gives us and the need in the world around us, and we keep putting it off. We are too tired or too busy; sometimes we set off in our own strength and go the hard way ending up exhausted really wishing that we had never decided to start in the first place; we are worn out and a million miles from being the peaceful example of one who has been born again with a living, loving, caring Jesus, and yet if we take time to pray and feed on God's Word, listen, and only do what He tells us to do we will arrive at His destination fresh, excited, and ready for more.

I received another revelation of a loving God and Father that weekend. Beryl and I have always enjoyed being together and enjoy the beauty and peace of the countryside. As we went for a walk just before setting off home I felt the Lord was telling me that these things fitted into His plan, but in much greater abundance when we are doing it for Him instead of for us. I believe on that weekend a vision was planted in me to set up a holiday home as an extension to the farm to provide holidays for those we helped at the farm so that they could compare for themselves the difference between the excitement of discos, night life, drugs etc and the beauty of the Welsh countryside.

Twelve months later we were back again. On this occasion I woke early on the Saturday morning and had a clear picture not of a huge expensive house but a little cottage with a small barn beside it. The cottage would be used by our extended family, the barn used to store tents and camping equipment, and the grass could be used for youth clubs camping while the leaders could use the cottage.

It was so clear and I got really excited and shared it with Beryl as we drove to Pwllheli for the day. Whilst walking around the shops we passed an Estate Agent and there in the window was a picture of the cottage I had seen that morning. I was completely stunned. It being a Saturday they were closed so we put a note through the letterbox asking for details. A few days later they arrived at home and it was just as I had seen it but the price was £39,000. Where would the money come from? So I filed the information and forgot about it. A few days later we were praying together when I realised we had made a serious mistake. God had given us a vision - He had turned that vision into a reality. We had again put this in the little box of our faith (or lack of it) because of the money so we started to pray that if He wanted us to buy it He must show us where the money was coming from.

We only shared this with a few friends because the idea was so way out and there were also the repairs of the barn to pay for but as a result of that sharing two business men offered to loan the money subject to the building being sound.

I need hardly say that God and our faith in Him grew quite considerably. We phoned the Estate Agent and arranged to visit the property on the following Sunday. We contacted the nearest church which happened to be church of England. It was close by and we were told was 'into renewal'. We explained our purpose and said we would join them for worship on Sunday.

On Friday, the Estate Agent phoned to say the property was sold. WHY?? We may never know the whys but there is always a lesson to learn. I confess I was a little relieved because we were not ready to take on another project at that time, but God had certainly shown us how He can move if we trust Him in all things. Now some thirty odd years later our vision has come to pass, not as a cottage in Wales but in the form of a 6 berth caravan in North Derbyshire. God knew all along His plan for us and all He asked of us was to trust Him. Joni Eareckson put it well when she said, *"We may not know the whys but we do know who has the answers."* So many stop when they cannot understand, and yet we must have faith in the God who holds us.

At that time in our lives God seemed to speak to us in so many different ways. There were pictures, the quiet still internal voice, a stranger, or a prayer partner who shared with us what the Lord had to say. One of the clearest was on 4th September 1986. We were at a YFC service with possibly around five hundred people in the congregation.

I cannot remember a word of the message but at the end the preacher said, *"I have a picture of a young couple with a farm that God wants to use. It is a picture of an old black iron pump and five p's are trickling out of the spout."* WOW!!! We had an old black iron pump in our kitchen. From that day on we called it the 'Pump Fund'. Incidentally, when we left the farm we took the pump with us, it now lives in our garden.

I Want You to Meet My Jesus

Chapter II

Newsletters

On the title page of this book are four pictures of Jesus. My favourite one is the bottom left of a child snuggled into a big hand. Through our various experiences God has shown His Love for us in both large and apparently small ways.

After Christmas, the practical work on the barn came to a standstill again and so I had plenty of time to pray and study and build myself up.

In the January Beryl was approached by a double glazing rep in Hillard's and he came out to see the barn – of course we were dreaming and there was no way we could afford those sort of windows(!!!) Nevertheless he left us a quote for £2400. The next day the phone rang at 9.00am and it was 'BBC Children in Need'. I had written to them three months ago and forgotten all about it. They wanted to know what they could do to help; they did not just want to put money into the project but wanted to finance a particular part of the project up to £3000. Ding dong!! The Lord's timing again! They were quite happy to consider that and sent us an application form. I spent the rest of that day just praising and praying.

We were now sending out a regular newsletter which generated a lot of prayer and finance. Writing has always been one of my weak spots and I was quite dyslexic at school but somehow the newsletters just came to me, often in the middle of the night and it was like God was in my fingers.

I have included a few excerpts:-

"Things are moving very slowly in the barn. I am getting a bit of local help but we are waiting for the YTS to turn up. It seems a very strange set up and no-one is prepared to make any decisions or promises."

On 21st January I write - "God has given us so much. We must share it."

On Monday 10th February the YTS turned up and we spent another week of frustration waiting for tools to arrive and get the canteen set up. Finally work did start and although painfully slow, we hoped that the lads would benefit from working on the barn but this was not to be. The work was really too complicated and varied and the lads got out of hand. In fact we decided to part company on 26th March.

Prophecy at a planning meeting -

"Your plans will be my plans and my plans will be your plans; you will pick the fruit and reap the harvest.

Do not be afraid but be aware; be concerned and be prepared to work. Lay your fear with Me and leave it there – a difficult time is coming, put your hand in mine and I will lead you.

You are trying to see, do and organise too much; you are obedient but at times you are reluctant and are obedient because you do not have any choice.

The evangelism will evolve, it will not be contrived.

Concentrate on building up the barn into a home; Roger's job is to look after the farm, home, and family – he is the father of the home and that is his job."

"That was written thirty five years ago – things seem to have got worse!! Over the past few months a particular Bible passage has spoken to us in Matthew 11:27-32 - in which there is a storm and Jesus is seen to be walking on the waves. Peter, who is in the boat, says "Call me Lord and I will come." Jesus did call him and he got out of the boat. Whilst he kept his eyes on Jesus he was ok, but when he looked at the waves that surrounded him he began to sink. For most of our lives we have been happy and comfortable to sit in the boat but with the barn the Lord has called us to what appeared to be an impossible task – to convert an old crumbling ruin (that's the barn not us) into something beautiful for Him, to be used by Him, when we had no money or experience. As soon as we got out of the boat the waves were enormous - doubts about where everything would come from and discouragement from the most unexpected sources. But whilst we kept our eyes on Jesus all things just came together in the most wonderful and sometimes miraculous ways. We have doubted many times and looked at or listened to the waves and we have started to sink very quickly, but as soon as we looked back to Jesus we were ok – we thank you again for your prayers that lift us up at these times."

"It seems incredible that in November we had not started. The new roof was on by December and even though we threw many broken tiles away we still had enough to re-roof it with six to spare. The internal upstairs floor is now finished and we have been given a table tennis table - God's attention to detail again - so the games room (the upper room!!) is now cold but functional; although there aren't any stairs as yet."

"We have altered the plans a little so that the downstairs accommodation doors will be wide enough for a wheelchair and make it more versatile."

We were introduced to a young unemployed Christian whose previous job had been timber preservation. So we laid hands on him, and he came one Saturday and treated all the old timbers in the barn and the rest of the buildings that we had not even started yet – God's attention to detail as that would not have occurred to me. The old beams were full of wood worm and God had provided a professional in a miraculous way. The work was going ahead steadily and there was a bit of money in the bank, but we were using it up quite quickly.

At that time I knew we should be getting quotes for other jobs and another quote for the 'Children in Need 'grant. It was quite surprising the variation in price for the double glazing and it was soon very clear that the best was most expensive. Why should God not have the best? This did cause a bit of conflict with our prayer partners, but we were expecting to provide accommodation for young mums and new born babies through CARE. The place, with fierce cold winds, was not called Highfields for nothing.

We kept praying for guidance and got it in different ways – we were continually reminded of God's promises to provide but we had to be sure. In the end we ordered what He wanted us to order.

I read a book at that time about a group of German nuns that were building a church. They needed a lot of bricks to finish it. They prayed for two years and then had a revelation that they should order the bricks and trust in the Lord's provision. Sure enough, when the lorry arrived with the bricks the postman also arrived and in the post was enough money to pay for their order of bricks.

(I hesitate as now thirty-five years later I can hardly believe this happened.)

At the same time as reading this wonderful story, I discovered that the manager of our first choice for the double glazing was an ex Baptist Minister. I phoned him and he came to see us. After explaining the situation we asked if he would accept the order knowing that we had not got the money to pay – he said that was "ok" so the order was placed. A lot of prayer went into that decision and I would not have felt right about it without giving him an explanation.

The Sales Manager of British Gypsum came to see us on 16th March (I had written to him). He was impressed with the project and said he would let us know what they could do to help. A few days later we received a letter from them asking us to arrange transport for five tons of plasterboard. The next day also at this time three local lads offered to help me on odd days. So things started to move again, the internal walls started to grow, and it began to look less like a barn and more like a house. The Saturday morning prayer meeting was beginning to grow and the Methodist Youth Club at Spondon started to take a keen interest on Saturdays, so things began to happen more quickly. It is impossible to remember all the little and big things that happened. Most people would call them 'coincidences', but we didn't have such wonderful times before we came to know Jesus and so for us they truly were His miraculous provision.

There was a memorable occasion on one Saturday. The whole youth club had begun to re-roof the second part of the barn and had come in for a well-earned cup of tea. They had been asking where the tiles were coming from as there were clearly not enough. There was a knock on the door and there was a customer asking for a bag of potatoes. He saw that the roof was being re-tiled and asked if we needed any more tiles as there were 3,000 just being taken off of a barn where he worked. Wow that's my Jesus!!

The Lord never let us down and working with young people as we did, He repeatedly did things like that just to thrill and encourage us and to physically let us know He was still with us. His timing is so wonderful.

I Want You to Meet My Jesus

Chapter 12

A Historical Note.

I want to share a little historical note.

The date in the wall of the barn is 1742, and we had been told that many years ago the timbers in the roof had come out of a ship. In fact, at the time of the building of the barn it was illegal to cut a tree down and the penalty was death (so I understand) so the settlers took their boats to bits and reused the timbers.

I had been unable to imagine how these odd shapes of wood could fit into a boat, but on a visit to see my dad we went to Southampton to see the hulk of the Mary Rose that had been dug out of the Solent - and there were the timbers similar to ours.

1986 At this time we received several prophetic words. I have included one below:-

7th December 1986 at church; Pastor Oliver Eley.

"I am allowing you to pass through the fires of difficulty, disappointment, and loss, so that, as the silver and gold is refined by fire, you too will come forth purified and more precious to me.

As you go out weeping, bearing the precious seed of my word and Spirit, so according to my word you will return rejoicing and bringing your sheaves with you.

I will surely bless you and your work."

Ray Scorey came into our lives at this point, sent to us by Hollybush. Ray was to become a close family friend and led our prayer meetings for several years. It is amazing how God works and provides but first we have to need!! And pray, and trust.

There are a lot of entries in my diary around this time. We were involved with a lot of young people and having serious problems with our neighbour down the drive.

1986 Diary excerpts:-

January 1986 - "Had a bad night all about overdrafts and finances - I clearly had not learnt to trust. Very excited about something this week: something is going to happen."

"No money for food or heating - just trusting enough for each day and it happens.

We were asked to resign as steward and sunday school teacher as our fellow Christians could not accept that God had spoken to us. We moved on and were again asked to leave"

23rd May 1986 - "It's official. No notices about Highfields to be given out at church and the minister was not happy about the existence of the ECF."

The minister left shortly after that, but the evening before he left he came to see us. "I have come to apologise – I knew you were right but didn't have the courage to stand up for you." We loved that man and suggested that the church he was moving to may give him similar problems.

"We were sitting round the table talking about the Marathon – Jane laughed and said I didn't stand a chance, so I put my shorts on and got to the bottom of the drive and back. Well I was not fit was I? The next day I got up to the crossroads and back and realised I could possibly do the half-Marathon and raise some money for the barn. My runs got longer. In the car I measured different routes including running home from church on Sundays. It's amazing what you can do if you make the effort and if it's for God the limits are endless – oh and I did raise £700 for the barn."

22nd June 1986 - "Jane cut herself again. This had happened several times and was having a bad effect on our children both at home and at school. She was in hospital, and we told her social worker that we could not have her back. She pleaded with us and we agreed just one more time, but Jane was seriously awful. On one occasion we had a row whilst washing up and I poured the washing up water over her head, scrambled egg in her hair, me full of shame.

The next day I was taking the children to school and asked her if she would like to come for the ride. On the way back I said, "What are we going to do Jane?" She replied, "I want to give your Jesus a try." Well I cried all the way home. Beryl cried when we got home and Jane was transformed from an angry overweight teenager to a beaming happy one, so much so that when her social worker next called she did not have to say a word. "My goodness Jane what's happened to you? "she asked, "I have decided to become a Christian" was the reply. The social worker responded by saying, "Oh dear, I will have to act as the devil's advocate."

She sat down at the kitchen table and explained that when she went back to school her friends would laugh at her and ended up talking her out of her decision."

At the classes we went to in order to become foster parents we were told to encourage anything positive, so this made no sense to us.

Sadly, things got bad again and we had to ask her to leave. We were told we must not contact her but leave it to her to make contact with us. Some months later on Jane's birthday we went to where she was living. When she saw us she ran into our arms asking, "why didn't you keep in touch?" We asked her the same question but she had been told the same thing as us – not to contact us, but to leave it to us.

We did keep in touch and years later she became our first van driver, got married had children and we still enjoy a loving relationship with her.

4th July 1986 - "We hosted the annual Methodist Association of Youth Clubs camp. On the Saturday evening we had a concert of items from visiting clubs which was a lot of fun and then the epilogue led by John Pickering, a local evangelist. He was a brilliant singer/song writer, singing some general songs as well as some Christian songs too. At the end he asked us all to stand and we sang "Let there be love shared among us." there are no words to describe the next few moments - it was like the marquee was on fire.

John acknowledged that something was happening, and he sensed there were youngsters who wanted to give their lives to the Lord. He spoke this out and asked us all to sit down unless you were one of those people – thirty youngsters remained standing. There had been no religious build up, just a sovereign act of the Holy Spirit. Even now John says that that never happened to him ever before or since.

If you have ever led a youth camp you will know how hard it is to get everyone off to bed, but on this occasion there were little groups outside each tent just quietly praying. "

12ᵗʰ July 1986 - "Open Day and Rally, 400 came."

28ᵗʰ July 1986 - (This is my last entry for quite a long time - our experience of valleys and hills, even of depression - so I write word for word from my diary) "Seriously hard times - since the camp and the rally I am close to a nervous breakdown. Our pastor came to see me: *"Stop trying to take on God's problems."*

During mid-1986 and through 1987 there was not much progress and we felt for most of that period that we were learning to be patient and that prayer is not always answered to our time table.

In early 1986 we felt sure we were nearly there and the 'real work' would begin. But what was the 'real work'? Rebuilding the barn? Raising the money? Building relationships with people and governmental departments? Waiting for God? Now as I write I wonder if the real work had even started, and yet some incredible foundations had been laid.

I Want You to Meet My Jesus

Chapter 13

Things Came to a Standstill

Following the camp and the rally things just came to a standstill. We ran out of money and had no help – as God had promised to provide we had to ask him "why?" He had stopped so that we could put things right.

I witnessed that the project had become too important to me. It is easy to put all your effort into the building and raising money and forgetting the real work. I had begun to worship the building and He was not going to let me fall into that trap.

We also discovered we had not explained the project properly to our neighbours. All sorts of terrible rumours were going round about the sort of people that were living at Highfields. One lady, we were told, would not go out at night, and that was before the barn was even finished.

Due to the rumours and the unease felt by our neighbours we decided that it was important to explain and so we called on all the neighbours to do just that. I also had to get back to looking after the farm and put 'the barn' in its place instead of letting it rule me.

Isn't God gentle with His correction if we really seek to find our faults and with His help correct them? In my past life He had to be anything but gentle as I did not always want to hear Him.

Christmas came and still no work had been done in four months of inactivity with no money. I had made several attempts to start again but it was obvious that it was not right and so it was back to prayers and "Why Lord?"

I felt sure at this time that God was challenging people to give money to the barn but nothing came – was I imagining it or was I once again standing in the way of answered prayer? We were to discover later that quite a large amount of money was paid out to us by a charity, but the cheque never reached us and was paid into a private bank account. This really did test our belief that to love people was more important than the building, and forgiveness must come as naturally as Jesus forgave even while He was on the cross.

Surprisingly, I felt really sorry for the guy when he confessed to us, and even many years later it still stung a bit. In the end we decided we would not get involved with any legal implications.

It had been a good year in many ways because I had seen what God could do even though I did get in the way from time to time.

Money did start to come in again in usable quantities after Christmas and we felt a real peace about starting work again. We had grown spiritually in many directions, and I had taken on a part time job for four months which had helped us as a family, especially during the Christmas season.

Work on the barn itself did not progress at any great pace from December 1986 to March 1987, but the monthly planning meetings really got to work and from them a whole series of summer evangelistic rallies were arranged, to be available as a means of outreach to all churches. The atmosphere at each meeting was terrific and every month new faces appeared.

Again we were being shown that the building was only a very small part of His work. Telling people about Jesus is what we should be all about and that seemed to be happening just as much while we were working on the construction as it would be when the barn would be completely finished.

It may have felt God had been on a go slow but He has a wonderful way of reminding us that He will never leave us or forsake us, and that He will show us a light for the path we are on.

Chapter 14

"Oh Dear God, Where Have You Gone?"

Diary excerpt 1986 -

"Oh Dear God, where have you gone to?"

"Suddenly my business is not doing so well, the unpaid bills are piling up, we haven't had many customers and wonder if we can even afford to advertise. There seems to be a tension and upset at home and temptations of all kinds are just crowding in."

Where was that God I had so recently felt so close to?

I guess every Christian has felt this at some time or another and it is almost the first shock to hit us after we have committed our lives to God. People can often paint such a wonderful picture of a life of ease and comfort (a bed of roses). Many books too gloss over the testing times and on many occasions these periods have led us to believe that really it is a big con and maybe the truth is not true after all. Where is God in those times?

For much of my searching years I wanted to believe that the book of Job did not belong to the Bible, that a kind and gentle God could not let those things happen to us His children. This impression was brought about by a few serious misconceptions in my faith.

First of all this life on earth is very short in relationship to eternity and no matter what happens to us here, if we truly follow God's way then we WILL go to heaven. Jesus has prepared a place for us in His Father's mansion; again we must trust our Jesus for that and gladly accept all that comes our way in this life. He has promised to never leave us or forsake us.

Secondly it is in times of trouble or stress when Christians show others how strong their faith is and the value of our relationship with Jesus – if we get irritable or allow our circumstances to dictate our behaviour and mood then we have missed the point somewhere. That is that in fact God is there all the time, especially in the testing times and the difficult circumstances.

How many of us think we have faith and trust God until a testing time arrives? Try to remember the key – have you got the peace? If you have not then go back and find it; remembering when you last felt it; go back to where 'your axe was sharp'.

As for Job the Bible tells us that one of the gifts of the Spirit is faith and some are blessed with the most amazing faith as in fact Job was. Don't get the idea that God causes bad things to happen. They are just part of living in the world. God's promise is to help us deal with them. Remember the end of Job's life was better than the beginning.

1987 - "What does God want me to do?"

This is a question we all ask but before we get the answer He has to be sure of our love for Him. And also we must learn to LISTEN – it takes time and patience to interpret answers from God as they come in so many different ways, through our trusted friends, through the Scriptures, through a word or prophecy, through a witness in our spirit and sometimes through an audible voice.

I have learnt that He WILL provide for His work in our lives, but if we dash off and do good things because it seems like the right thing to do then we will pay the price in energy and finance, and so it is better for us to be obedient. This often involves NOT doing things. We need to listen and if we get tired or weary then we need to take time out to pray and maybe ask what we shouldn't be doing. The 23rd Psalm tells us that we will be led beside still waters to be refreshed. Sometimes we think that God can't manage without us, or we ask ourselves "can we trust Him that if we do not do a certain thing then He has chosen another way to do it?" Our interference can often slow the work down.

We must remember to step back and Let God be God especially in how we pray and what we ask for. If we choose to just pray for every need and every hurt then our prayers become a meaningless list. It is important for us to choose to take time to listen and allow our spirit to direct us in how we pray and what we should pray for. It is likely that we may even become part of the answer.

This is what I have learnt during this time.

Guidance is an area in which we all make mistakes and an area in which I am not qualified to give much help. I have made so many wrong moves, have taken sincere advice without asking God or just taken no advice and done things my own way. I have come to understand that we are to look to the Lord for guidance bringing everything to the Lord in prayer.

It is impossible for me to say how we came to recognise this guidance but there is a peace that passes all understanding and that is given at the right time – and yet I still make mistakes!!

When we decide to move forward in a direction then, it is important to do it slowly and prayerfully ensuring that we check each move for peace, always being prepared to stop or change course. This is not an excuse to stop. God will reveal His purpose for us when He knows we are ready to listen and to follow Him.

I Want You to Meet My Jesus

Chapter 15

God Knows What We Need

For some years I had been told about and heard tapes from 'Spring Harvest,' a large gathering of Christians of all ages from all over the country that meet together for one week of the year.

We had often said that we would like to go but as our house was always full of people passing through we preferred to spend our holidays as a small family and enjoy our quality time together.

However in 1987 we decided to give it a try and along with two other families from Etwall we booked to go to Skegness.

During the latter part of the winter of 1986/7 I had spent hardly any time on the barn, due to both the weather conditions and the lack of money, so I concentrated my efforts on our little farm. We had a small flock of ewes and purchased twenty four calves which we often did, to rear and sell as weaned calves to beef farmers.

As March came to an end we had finished lambing and needed to sell the ewes and lambs. Also the calves were ready to sell, but the winter was still with us and nobody wanted to buy what we had to sell.

There were frantic phone calls to markets and dealers. The feed bill was escalating and I was extremely worried as we were due to go to Spring Harvest in two weeks' time and all at home was chaos. We had arranged for a family to come and stay at the farm in our absence, but they were expecting to come for a restful holiday.

One morning as I was feeding the stock, the rain was pouring down and I felt very troubled. Suddenly it seemed as if I had walked through a wall of peace. A voice said, *"They are my animals; you look after them and I will move them in my time not yours."* Needless to say we had prayed a lot before taking on the sheep and the calves. We had also prayed a lot since, and here I was thinking I knew best or that God would let us down. We often realise, or it seems, that God is the God of the last minute, but it is His way of testing our faith. Well I started to whistle and praise the Lord. I was at peace. Then a name and a price came into my head. I phoned the name that I knew who handled a lot of sheep. Yes he did have some spare grass. He came round, offered me the right price, phoned for a lorry and they were all gone within six hours leaving me with a cheque in my pocket.

The next day an enormous cattle lorry came into the yard. The driver asked for me as he had been told I had some calves to sell. He told me that he had a customer desperate for twenty weaned beef calves. Well he bought them and I was left weak and ashamed because of all my fretting and worrying, instead of trusting in God!

The next day Beryl and I were sorting potatoes when 'crack' went my back and I slumped down on a sack of potatoes, my legs numb. I asked Beryl to pray for me, but as we prayed I felt sure that I was not to be healed there and then, but that God was going to use my pain for His Glory, and I felt a sense of peace wash over me.

This meant that the week before we were due to go I was laid out with a slipped disk even though I had the enormous job of cleaning out the calf sheds before we left for our holiday.

The next morning I looked out of the window and there was a friend of mine. A young Christian, knowing of my plight, decided that he would get on with it for me. I hobbled outside in amazement, and he said he would like to come in and pray with me as he had a lot of problems. Although he was self-employed he had little work to do.

We had a great time together which I believe would not have taken place if he had not felt called to come and help me out. So my backache had opened a door and I began to realise that we are also part of other peoples' journey too.

Diary excerpts from that time -

"A new lad came to us, who was badly disabled with fingers on each elbow and a steel pin in his back. He had a condition called thalidomide. He arrived after breakfast, and we had a cup of coffee and a long chat as I really did not feel like work. I told him about 'Miracle Valley' and the Hollybush Youth Camp. He was so open and keen I asked him if I could pray with him before we started work and he said "Yes." That was a miracle in itself as I have not got to that stage in two years with some people.

I held his fingers and prayed for both of us. He told me "Something" had happened and we had a great day together. I was the one hobbling around, while he was rushing about following my instructions."

"Another meeting in the barn followed, this time it was part of a series on counselling. On this occasion the title was 'Victorious Living'. Even surrounded by so many miraculous situations we ashamedly did not feel very victorious. I shall always remember the message. Victory is not getting rid of the situation but being victorious in it.

At the end of the meeting a lady who had been praying for the boy with thalidomide shared that he had been round to her house since coming to the farm and told her he was going to 'Miracle Valley Youth Camp', after a conversation with me. He told her he was going to get some new arms, and a friend of his who has a glass eye has asked if he could go too. My instant reaction was "Oh no, what have I said?" I knew I had not suggested he go for that, but I did tell him about my Jesus, so I knew I must leave it to God to lead the way."

Chapter 16

Spring Harvest

Our first trial of faith was when Butlins wrote back to say that the basic self-catering accommodation was fully booked. They could only offer us a luxury apartment costing an extra fifty pounds for the week. As we were determined to give it a try, although unsure how we would cope with luxury or find the extra fifty pounds, we booked. God was beginning to teach us that He wanted the best for us and provided.

Three days to Spring Harvest - The doctor came to see me (yes he did in those days) and could find nothing wrong with me! "Oh well it couldn't have been a slipped disc but I'll give you a sick note for another two weeks." What a mighty God we have – a miracle healing and full pay whilst at Spring Harvest!!

One day to Spring Harvest - Nicky comes home from school with a badly swollen throat, headache, and tummy ache. Well that's it. We were really weary by this time and hardly had the energy to do any more praying or casting out demons or anything else. But of course we did pray and asked a few others to pray as well. We phoned the doctor and he agreed to meet us ten minutes before surgery the following morning. The day arrives and yes our God has not let us down. Nicky was fine. I took her rather sheepishly to the Doctors as agreed and although there was a little redness in her throat there was nothing wrong with her. Miracles do have rather embarrassing sides sometimes but who is complaining, and our God has seen us through the obstacle course. We were ready to go expecting great things after all this aggro.

How God copes with us or why he even tries is a mystery to me, but He is a great Father and like any Father likes to help us even when we make silly mistakes. We had been told to take 50pence pieces with us for the meter, and when we left home my trousers were so weighed down with change I gave half of it to Beryl, who promptly paid one of the lads to reduce the weight in her bag. We stopped at a Little Chef on the way and I paid the bill with 50pence pieces – is it possible to be so stupid? So imagine us cold, wet, muddy falling through the door and realizing the only way to heat the place was to put 50pence pieces in the meter. Oh no!! We searched our pockets and had one 50p each so I put the first one in the meter. It fell out the bottom and all the heating came on. For the rest of the week we only needed that one 50p. I hasten to add that we did report the fault to the office but no one came to put it right.

Writing these things out now they seem so small but at the time they were major miracles and a simple demonstration of God's presence and love for us.

Two hours later the entire Butlins complex was plunged into darkness, later we were to discover, due to a massive overload. Water was fed to the taps by an electric pump so again imagine ten thousand people in a strange place, cold wet and muddy after a long journey, in darkness and no water. After a further two hours some emergency lighting was on in the office and the wind and rain were still in full force, so we decided to go into 'Skeggy' for a warm up and a Chinese meal – two restaurant meals in one day and one third of our money gone!

We got back to the apartment at 9.30pm. There was still no power so I went to the reception to find out what was happening. I was immediately aware of a wonderful atmosphere. The Butlins girl behind the desk was weary from explaining, but even she must have sensed the joyful peaceful atmosphere of those come not to complain but to find out the situation. I was told the fault was big with no chance of any power before tomorrow. So our family went to bed in our clothes shivering and cold but remembering to pray for those who were working to restore things.

Have you ever felt so miserable that you just want to talk to someone? You know all your thoughts are wrong but for some reason you just want to wallow in it. As a Christian you know there is a way out but you stubbornly refuse to take it. Well I record the next few days in detail of how we were back then and the lessons learned and to show in the details of God's wonderful patient love for us. Let me set the scene for you.

For those who have never been to Spring Harvest you buy a programme and find that there are so many seminars each day that the choice is endless obviously catering for all tastes; there are also lots of other things going on including the most amazing facilities for children to release parents so they can join in the seminars. As it was our first time we decided we would not force Nicky and Kelly into the children's programme - only to go if they were happy to do so.

Sunday, day two of our stay and Praise the Lord! The power had been restored. The children had both willingly gone to their children's area and we were off to the 'Big Top'. We were so expectant that God would do great things for us. He was going to revive our spirits and bless our socks off for all the problems we had come through - after all we felt He owed us a break.

We collected the children at lunch time. Kelly threw herself into my arms crying. Someone had been unkind to her and she was definitely NOT going again. We had promised to take them to the Fun Splash swimming pool that afternoon feeling sure this would cheer her up, but the queue was so long that it was out of the question. It seems silly afterwards when you see how tempers get edgy, but we doggedly kept praying and expecting God to bless us.

That evening was 'Songs of Praise' in the Big Top, the first time it had been recorded live for fifteen years. It was a remarkable experience; we watched it on the telly in our apartment as we were not able to take the children in with us.

Monday came and we had made up our minds not to force the children to do anything or get hang-ups about going to seminars. One of the children was not co-operating and didn't want to fit in with our plans, so Beryl decided to take Kelly staying with her for the morning. I took Nicky to her activity and couldn't help but laugh about a further frustration. She had been allocated to a group called the 'Little Burgers'. It was a wonderful idea as nine hundred children had been split into small groups and all given a name, and a flag to wave over the group, helping parents to find the correct one. The project for that day was to paint the flag. As we were a little late we went into this enormous room crammed with groups of children but no flags. Each flag had come down and was smothered with bodies with paint brushes. So valiantly I set out. "Has anybody seen the Little Burgers?" No-one was listening to me. There seemed to be hundreds of groups and I kept calling for the Little Burgers.

I found the group, left Nicky, and went off to the morning Bible study. At coffee-time I went to see Beryl and Kelly but things were not well. We decided Kelly was not going to be happy in her children's group and took her out. Again it sounds silly now but we were both close to tears. It felt as if our break with all our hopes was going wrong; God wasn't giving us the break we felt we deserved. We went to the office and found a lovely man who came and counselled us. He suggested we should arrange for Kelly to become a 'Little Burger' with Nicky.

In the afternoon we made it into the Fun Splash and had a great time. One of our friends from Etwall agreed to baby sit so we could go to the evening celebration. Things were looking up; when we got back there was a note to say Kelly was now a 'Little Burger'. Praise the Lord we were on our way.

The following day we told Kelly there was a letter for her. Nicky then went into a deep sulk as there was not a letter for her too. Parents, I hope will understand that these apparently trivial things can knock you over very quickly. Soon we were all falling out with each other, Beryl was not feeling very well and we hit the bottom again – "This isn't fair God! We came for a break."

I am embarrassed to recall our time at the breakfast table, Nicky, who was aged seven at the time saying, "Can we all sit on the settee and pray, then start the day again?" Sadly Beryl and I ignored the comment and yet what a wonderful pearl of wisdom that was, and what made it worse was that we knew she was right. It was decided that no-one wanted to be a Little Burger that morning so Beryl stayed with the children and I went off to the Bible study.

I was in a real mess so I went to seek some prayerful help rather than go to the Bible Study. I knew that Doug Barnett was leading the management team of Spring Harvest. I had not seen him since I went forward twenty six years before at the age of eighteen for the first time at a meeting led by him at Spicer Street Baptist Church. He was nowhere to be found. I went out into the street and cried to the Lord. I found myself using the words of Psalm 61. "*Hear my cry oh Lord, listen to my Prayer; from the ends of the earth I call to you; as my heart grows faint lead me to the rock that is higher than I."*

I decided to go back to the office and leave a message for Doug to contact me at our apartment. As I was writing the note someone came into the reception and there he stood the man I hadn't seen for twenty six years. God had heard my cry and used Doug to lead us back to the Rock. He asked if we were having a good time and was gracious enough to not look shocked when I said "no". He came back to the apartment with me and after talking for a while he realised that we were so used to living in tense situations and being able to handle them that we could not cope with normal family situations. Our children could not relate to us in this wonderful peaceful setting and nor could we relate to them. He explained that the way they were behaving was perfectly normal for children and we had come away with preconceived ideas of how God was going to bless us. We knew He was going to bless us but we were telling Him how to do it.

So it is with all the visions and promises that God gives us. They are real and He will provide them for us but in HIS way. If we start telling Him how to go about it then all comes to a standstill or goes wrong. We had told Him we deserved a rest; we had told Him how we wanted to be blessed.

We had a good time of prayer before Doug dashed off following his busy schedule. We decided to go for a drive to visit some Christian friends about thirty miles away. They were so pleased to see us and carried on where Doug left off. We then chose to put God first and allow Him to do what he wanted with us.

Day five and we sent two happy Little Burgers off to play leaving us free to go off to the Big Top, released and pliable in His hand. We had said sorry to each other and to Him our peace and joy restored. I found my spirit was so full of joy that I could not sing a word in the worship as the words of the choruses just ministered to me:-

"No condemnation now I dread, Jesus and all in Him is mine"

Then came the next verse:-

"It makes a wounded spirit whole, And calms the troubled breast."

Have you ever tried to sing when your Adam's apple is trying to get out of your throat? Why try to sing I decided, just let Jesus love me.

We had a lovely time with our friends from Etwall at lunch time and then went to the family film show in the Butlins cinema in the afternoon, followed by a great celebration in the evening, with another baby sitter in charge.

During our time at Spring Harvest we attended an evening celebration. The subject was on forgiveness and was led by Elizabeth Elliot. Her first husband had been speared to death by a tribe of Indians, who she later went to live with accompanied by her three-year-old daughter. Her second husband died in great pain from cancer. It was a very moving experience as many of the 4,000 present began to realise that there were areas of unforgiveness in our lives, or that we had not accepted ourselves. *"Is God's Grace not big enough for your sins?"* She likened it to a sea shell on the shore wondering if the ocean was big enough to fill it.

After a time of standing prayer she asked people to sit down if the Lord had shown an area of unforgiveness in their hearts. Beryl and I both sat down and Elizabeth asked those around to pray, although most were now sitting. But the prayers were giving release, and even sat among all those people, God was treating me as an individual – He was ministering to our personal needs, and even though 3,999 other people surrounded me, a lot of them were having that same personal one to one experience of their Father's love that I was.

Chapter 17

January 1988

Prophecy at church:-

"There have been many things that you have done which you have not understood, but you have been obedient, even in very small things. I have required your obedience, even without your understanding and I have been pleased with how you have responded to me. It is only in your total obedience even without your understanding that you will see me move as you have desired, and I will move. You will see me do mighty and miraculous things of which you have only, so far, dreamed of as you responded in your obedience. So do not be afraid to trust me as I am in control and have purposed many things for you; and all I have required you have begun to do, and there will be many moves of my Spirit which astound all that see and hear. Read Deuteronomy 11:13-25, Hebrews 10:35-36"

January 1988 - 'Work starts again on the second barn and we see little miracles. A plumber came to fit the bathroom, as well as paint and the people to put the paint on the walls also arrived."

At that time we had up to four formally homeless youngsters living with us and I was helping with a drop in centre at church. I was feeling quite depressed at that time and on the way home one day I had an argument with God. "These young people don't need table tennis and coke cola they need a JOB." At that point, my faith was limited to what I could imagine. I saw that the youngsters I was working with would encounter difficulties when it came to finding and holding down a job, as they would be seen as unemployable.

Sometime later I was looking out of my bedroom window and saw the next door neighbour building something. I went across to see him and found out that he was building a huge chicken shed. I asked if we could help and so we got to know him. When the first chickens arrived he asked if we would like to do the egg collecting. At that time we had a particularly unkempt young lad with us, filthy language, snotty nose, and no matter how often Beryl washed his clothes he was just filthy; however he did like collecting eggs.

One day he asked me if he could go on his own. I was not happy about this, but I asked the neighbour and he said it was "ok." So I took the young lad and taught him to count, fill in the graph and keep the records. That unkempt young man was transformed. He stopped swearing, wiped his nose and became a clean and pleasant young man. I had told God He couldn't find him a job! I didn't realise it then but 'Happy Hens' was soon to be born.

In 1988 a YTS group came to help us and stayed for many years. The supervisor was called Bill even though the young people from the YTS changed as time went by we got to know him. Over a hundred must have been involved over that time, helping us to finish the barn, building the chicken sheds and finishing the paddocks. At this time I was growing as a Christian and enjoyed working with them all and telling them about my Jesus.

One day I let myself down badly though. The boys behaviour had really got to me and I became very angry and I started swearing at them. The words used I was sure I had long since forgotten. I felt so bad inside that when they were due to leave for home I stuck my head through their van window and apologised. The next day Bill told me they had not stopped talking about me all day. "Why?" I asked him. "Well" he replied, "they have been sworn at all their lives but no-one has ever apologised before!"

Over the years since then I have often felt inadequate, wondering why on earth God chose me and I often felt like a bad Christian. But I remember that time and how God can use the bad bits of me to still speak to others. In my weaknesses He is strong.

It was also during that time that we had terrible problems with a neighbour and the driveway we shared with him. There was no doubt about it, we were bringing very undesirable characters on to the farm and a natural fear turned into some very nasty incidents with him. Then all of a sudden his house was up for sale. Needless to say we had prayed a lot and this seemed like the answer. Unfortunately however it was then taken off the market again.

Several years later we found out that a church in Derby had nearly bought it for a Bible school but decided not to because of the things that were happening 'up the drive!!!!' This was very disappointing. What a wonderful answer to prayer that would have been. And of course the old question "Why Lord did you let that happen?" With the house no longer up for sale there followed many horrible years of friction and bad situations.

The first barn was finished, and it sounds ridiculous but we did not know what to do with it. A man came to our door looking for a site to store machinery for building the Etwall bypass. We got talking about the barn and he offered to rent it from us as an office and tool store for £125 per week. That was a fortune but not what we felt it was for. However, as it was for only a few months we agreed. Sadly, some of our supporters were not happy with our decision, but we had discovered the Lord provides in many ways, and that there are many ways we can share our faith along the way. We had a great time with those road contractors. We had been well paid for the privilege, and with the money we were able to purchase curtains and carpets.

In 1988 my mum came back into our lives. She had left in 1947 and we had had very little contact with her. Her husband had since died, so my brothers and I decided we should go to Rye and see what we could do to help her. She came back home with me and it was like a real life fairy-tale.

Initially she tried to live with us but it was too noisy in our house for her, so she lived in a home nearby right up until she died. I remember those years as such a time of an unexpected blessing. God is brilliant! He is interested in every part of our lives.

I had the privilege of holding my mum's hand as she died, her last words to me had been, "are you happy Rog?" Soon after that she was gone and was not there anymore. Yet what had gone? If her body had been weighed before and after the weight would still be the same. It was her spirit that had gone and she was now with Jesus.

I Want You to Meet My Jesus

Chapter 18

The Birth of Happy Hens.

In October 1988 we started to build our first 2,500-bird chicken shed and 'Happy Hens' was born. We remembered my sister's picture in 1985 of the yard covered in hens and wondering what God had meant!! I also remembered telling God these young people "need jobs not table tennis and coke cola".

Collecting Eggs in the Neighbour's Shed.

Alan had opened my eyes to the potential of teaching counting eggs *("cor f'in ell mister, how many eggs have we just collected?")* reading, writing, production graphs, and as the eggs came along so did a whole new ministry. It was not long before shed number two was built, then three, four, five, six and seven with 24,000 hens. Beryl said, at the time "Any more and I am leaving!"

The business model for 'Happy Hens' was amazing. We had paid work and education for our young visitors and all our supporting churches wanted to become egg agents. On one occasion I spoke at a 'Harvest Supper' and a lady came up to me and said, "I will sell your eggs." Within weeks she and her husband were taking ninety dozen a week. With a small mark up, in their first year their church received £1,200 profit. At another church a teenage girl, who was doing a paper round to save money to visit relatives in Canada, became an egg agent for her church and neighbours and was able to raise enough money to go to Canada. A housebound lady also became an agent. We delivered one hundred and eighty dozen every two weeks to her. She was able to give £400 to the Methodist Missionary Society every so often.

I could write a book of all the special stories relating to the egg sales, they were all a ministry on their own. The bonus was that all those hundreds of customers were hearing about what God was doing for troubled teenagers at 'Happy Hens.'

Prophecy from Hollybush Farm 24th November 1989 -

We were going through a particularly difficult patch and decided to go up to Hollybush and spend the day with Jim Wilkinson. It was Friday so we stayed on for their weekly open service. Jim shared our problems with the congregation and we were invited to the front for prayer and the following was spoken over us by Carl Gidney.

"You are to be an ice breaker. I see in my spirit that you are something like an ice breaker, like an ocean liner, that you will go where other people fear to tread that's right, to boldly go where others fear to tread, and that as you come against the coldness of God's frozen people there is sharpness – you are the cutting edge.

The Lord says, *"do not be afraid to launch out into those areas of coldness, those areas of barrenness where no-one else goes. For you are the ones who will be on the cutting edge, who will feel the pain but who will break the coldness and will break the ice and will be the ones who will pioneer, who will explore. Pioneers suffer. They pay the price."*

But the Lord says, *"do not struggle, just snuggle up closely to Him, warm your hearts and His warmth will break the coldness, will break the ice as you launch out."* *And as you do that I see coming behind you many other tugs that you will be pulling along behind you, other people; that as this area and this territory, this barren territory of hardness and harshness, of coldness and barrenness and desolation you break open, others will go off into other avenues; as the ice and the territory begins to break others will follow you; they follow at a distance, but the Lord is looking for people who have the Spirit, to have this Spirit, where others fear to go.*

Fear not, you are not like Elijah who said he was the only one left. The Lord has many whose hearts He has touched; you are not the only ones; you are not alone. He will join them to you and they will attach themselves to you but they will be behind you, and you will tug them along, but continue to venture," says the Lord"

Much of that was quite uncomfortable – 'to break the frozen heart of God's people' – who wants to hear that?

Chapter 19

Dad and Richard

1989 -

Dad and Elaine had decided to move to Tenerife and were due to sign a contract for a flat however none of us wanted them to leave. He had chosen to live in a warmer place but had a massive heart attack the day before. The contract did not get signed and he very nearly died. My brothers, sister and I went to see him in hospital and in true style we read Psalm 23 and did all the right things, saying good bye to him. The nurse told us all to go home at mid-night and promised she would phone us if there were any developments.

The next morning I rushed to the hospital and there was dad sitting up reading the Financial Times. I cried and said, "I wish I could take you home with me, dad." His reply was "I wish you could too."

A few weeks later we hired an ambulance and he came home to the barn where he and Elaine settled down to live. I looked after them for four years until he needed to go into a home where he died peacefully in 1995. Those years were the most precious I had spent with him and I am so thankful to Jesus for such a treasured time. Dad and Elaine sold their house in Hampshire when they moved in and were able to give us £60,000 to cover the cost of restoring the second part of the barn.

Prophecy from a friend April 1990 -

"Roger my son you are precious in my eyes, your every part is my pleasure.

Do not be afraid my son for you are never alone; even when the multitude have gone and you stand with no one by your side you are not alone.

And when the tasks that are before you seem to be impossible then you will be strong, for at times of great difficulty you will allow my presence to grow in your life; our relationship will grow stronger and stronger so that you will grow stronger and stronger. Listen to my words and feel my love around you and you will know my peace in your every moment."

By this time the first part of the barn was finished. Dad and Elaine were living in it. Dad had given us £60,000 to finish the second part of the barn and a trust from North Derbyshire came into our lives. They had a huge vision for working with young people. A couple of their trustees were elected to come and live at the farm in a caravan and supervise the restoration of the second part. Money was no longer a problem. The roof and damp proofing had already been done and they fitted the windows and internal walls, kitchen and bathrooms using professional help where required. Now the whole barn was seriously ready for action!

In 1992 on my fiftieth birthday Richard had another terrible accident. He was knocked off his bike and run over by a lorry. His spine and pelvis were broken in several places and there was a lump sticking out of his head. He couldn't possibly survive those injuries.

They stabilized him in Burton Hospital and then moved him to Oswestry spinal unit where he was on traction for seven weeks. We visited him every week and at the end of that time we went to the hospital to see the traction removed and to be told he would never walk again. That was one of the darkest moments of my life. We had during that time learnt that most of the people on the ward were motor-cyclists and a high proportion would end up committing suicide.

After many weeks Rich came out of hospital and went to live with his mum, later getting married and giving us two beautiful granddaughters. He is still on crutches but always has a huge smile on his face. We are all so proud of him.

My dad moved into a home around 1994 and the Trust purchased the barn and farmhouse. It was soon filled with youngsters and staff. Unfortunately, it was not long before things went wrong. The Trust had taken on a huge project in North Derbyshire nearer to their base and Highfields was not generating any income. We could not understand why but they did not want to help with the chickens, so we had to employ a full staff. They decided to move out and allowed us to raise the money to buy it back.

Then came another Trust with the same vision and again there was the same problem. They needed to generate the income to finance it. By then we had a team of staff to run the farm and the hens so they too moved out. This was a such a blow. Then in 2002 our problems were finally solved - BETEL!!!

WE WOULD BUILD IT AND OTHERS WOULD RUN IT.

Betel have their own amazing story but in short they are an amazing organisation in England and abroad. They are a rehab but much more than a rehab – more a school for evangelism. Whenever I go there to visit or to a service my eyes fill with tears as I remember the collapsed roofs, broken windows, and broken floors – all the amazing answers to years of prayer – and yes all the tears.

We have an amazing, patient God. His ways are not our ways and our ways are not His ways.

"The barn is finished, Betel has moved in and put the finishing touches to it. We claim the prophecy from 1985 that we would build it and others would run it. From now on that is their story."

I Want You to Meet My Jesus

Chapter 20

The Gideons (Now 'Good News for Everyone')

My first experience of the Gideons was in my twenties as a machinery rep and would spend a lot of time in hotels. One evening I really got stuck into reading the Bible and decided to take it home with me the next day. I didn't realise to many years later that it was not to be taken from the hotel and I had inadvertently stolen it.

I had been a Gideon for quite a while but I had always felt a bit of a misfit. I am not very comfortable with meetings and although overawed by the passion of my fellow Gideons I did not seem to fit. I did go with them to two of the many school presentations, but it was not really for me – I have always been a bit of a loner. Also the school assembly presentations were held at the same time as the students arrival at the farm making it hard to join my fellow Gideons.

We were always aware that we had to be careful not to push religion onto the children; however if a student asks, "How do you know there is a God?" - well then you are able to start a conversation about Jesus. There is never a stock answer as every situation is different, as every student is different but if I feel right about it, I give them a Personal Worker's New Testament. I gave one to a lad who when he next came to the farm said "Hey Rog, you know that Bible what you gave me? Well, I'm up to page 375!!"

Up to the late 1990's on the farm we did all our teaching in practical ways particularly in the chicken sheds. In the shop, there was the need for reading, writing, and dealing with customers. So our students were acquiring life skills in this way. Then we were introduced to a retired 'special needs' teacher David Hales, who on a voluntary basis introduced a more formal education and was with us until we finally closed down. Dave was a very faithful friend and prayer warrior and a brilliant teacher. Sadly he suddenly passed away in 2021.

On 1st January 2000 he came to our door and told me that he and his mates had been celebrating the New Year the evening before and decided they wanted to do something special for the new Millennium. They decided they were going to raise the money to build a classroom at Highfields. "But Dave" I said, "we don't need a classroom, this is a farm." "Well we are going to build one anyway." He replied. David was a very forceful character!

They decided to canoe from Ellesmere Port, Merseyside across the country to Boston in Lincolnshire. The Longford Community Challenge had been born. At the same time the schools had become more interested in our project and we had the reputation for getting really difficult youngsters back to school.

For us to become more official we needed to provide better facilities like a canteen, toilets, and a classroom. I had assumed we would get financial help to build what was needed. So I set about getting quotations for a new unit. When next I saw the teacher involved I told her it would cost £25,000. "Oh no, if you want to become official you have to finance it." We were shocked and so the Longford Community Challenge had suddenly become a necessity. How brilliant was that? God had already provided for all we needed. He is a good God!

The project grew rapidly with up to nine students a day. The classroom was in the canteen, which was proving difficult, so we decided to expand and to look round for a suitable second hand building. We found one in Chesterfield for £5,000 delivered and fitted. On the same day we had a visit from a local charity that had heard about our work who gave me a cheque for £5,000.

The Driveway - Angels come into our lives without us realising it.

Again at the end of the 1990's the Rural Development Grant was introduced. Our drive was all potholes and puddles so we applied for a grant to tarmac from Heage Lane to the shop for £35,000.

One evening after sending in our application I received a phone call telling us that our application had been rejected. He had phoned to tell me to reapply for tarmac all around the farm and call it wheelchair access. I duly sent in our renewed application for £128,000 and we were accepted transforming the farm. I truly believe an angel had phoned me.

Chapter 21

Bulgaria

I used to think that being a Christian would be very boring but my life was transformed once I met God. God gives guidance through the Bible and through people but more often it's a still small voice or a natural reaction to something out of the blue. I hasten to add that not all good ideas are God's ideas and they can involve a lot of soul searching and prayer. My best example was my time in Bulgaria.

A family in our church had become involved with a church in Krichim, Bulgaria, and were planning to take a lorry full of clothes, food, and medicines for the local hospital but they needed another driver. At the time I had a wonderful farm manager who was also a lovely Christian and wonderful with the students. He was more than happy for me to go, so for no particular spiritual reason I offered. There were four of us involved altogether and the date was fixed for us to leave. I and one other were to fly to Sophia, while the other two were to drive the lorry. The four of us were to distribute the clothes, food, and medicines, and then John and I would drive the empty lorry home.

With all the gifts and donations loaded, we took the lorry to a weighbridge and found that we were slightly underweight with lots of extra space. So Geoff and I went to Tesco and filled several trolleys with sanitary towels and toilet paper. The lady at the checkout gave us a funny look and asked if we had a problem!!

When I arrived in Bulgaria I looked around and saw hundreds of acres of weeds with thousands of starving people and being a practical farmer, I said "Please Lord let me meet a farmer." We went to the Gypsy village of Peristica and met pastor Salcho who owned thirty acres of weed-covered land. I told him I would go home and raise the money to buy him a tractor. We went to the local tractor dealer and got a quote for a tractor, trailer, and plough for £15,000.

It didn't take long to raise the money. Even the Bank Manager got excited and via him the money was sent to Salcho. Nearly a year later I went back and Salcho showed me a valley of vegetables – he told me "There will not be a hungry person in Perestica this winter." WOW!!

This is a great and happy memory that has stayed with me.

That was followed by our church raising the money to buy a small farm for our adopted church in Krichim – 'Happy Hens Krichim' was born. Which although it was hard work it was also an amazing experience. I had to go out several times to resolve various problems.

Sadly, the farm was not a success in some ways as the ex-communist mind was not used to making decisions. But it did have a huge positive effect on the young people I had come to know and love, as it was their first experience of work, and they went on to get other jobs. My experience of them on our first visit was bare feet in the snow. When I met them the last time they had leather jackets and shoes on.

Also around that time I was asked to provide some chicken equipment for an orphanage in Honduras, 'The Valley of The Angels'. Each country has its own special problems. In this case it was that the chicken run would have a scorpion problem. We filled a container with everything they could possibly need and off it went.

I Want You to Meet My Jesus

Chapter 22

A Struggling Time for Happy Hens

I confess I have recently struggled to write this book as there have been many times that the hens and the farm have taken over on my priority list.

We were living in the farmhouse with a rundown farm when we received the prophecies from Dr. Ann Townsend from CARE and from Hollybush. I had interpreted these for the house, barns, and farm so when the trusts started to take over and did not want to help with the chickens, we started a new venture based on my sister's picture of the 'farm covered in chickens'.

We already had four small sheds each with 2,500 birds and a huge hungry market for free-range eggs. Maybe this is when we made a big mistake at this point. We had made a considerable profit and decided to build two bigger sheds with 9,000 and 5,000 birds in each one. It had become a commercial enterprise by this stage. Yes it did create jobs but it needed a lot of experienced management with a lot more pressure on quality and marketing.

When we built our first shed, free-range eggs were not available in quantity until the supermarkets saw a new opportunity and began their relentless marketing to drive the price down. At that time I was a founder member of the British Free Range Egg Producers Association (BFREPA) in the naïve thinking that we could continue to market our own eggs through our own outlets. But the size of the shed became an issue and new sheds were being built and mechanised which drove the costs up and the price down – the BFREPA was and still is a huge success but unfortunately, the small producers got frozen out of the market.

All of our sheds were second hand and a bit rough, and as DEFRA (Department of Education, Food and Rural Affairs) and RSPCA imposed more stringent rules (our hens were happy and produced lovely big brown eggs at 90% production) it became impossible to keep up and eventually our sheds were condemned as unfit for egg production.

We were given time to do the necessary alterations or replacements most of which were impractical, but sadly I had a complete mental breakdown and was 'out of it' for six months – I had a good staff that kept things going and we had a few students passing through, but I could not go out of the house; in my head, it was all over. Every shed had a story - dismantled in different parts of the country, Doncaster, Redditch, Wales, Bristol, and bringing them home was a huge but fun job. We had a good and profitable outlet for our eggs but sadly we would have to close down.

In all of the difficulties and pressures I never stopped praying and reading my Bible at those times but maybe it was more out of habit or duty. I knew that He was always with me just patiently waiting for me to hold His hand again.

Trying to sort out what God is saying can be one of the most difficult parts of meeting my Jesus and a place where mistakes can be made, after all, it took us three years to realise that when He said chickens He meant chickens! Those mistakes are all part of the learning curve. You just need to keep looking to Him.

I Want You to Meet My Jesus

Chapter 23

Angry Hands to Gentle Hands

I was still going out speaking and had a good story to tell and although I was still feeling depressed, I had no doubt that God would do something. I was asked to speak at a church in Buxton. This was quite a long way from home which meant no-one would know me.

Afterwards a gentleman came to me and said, "I would like to help you". He came to the farm the next day, had a walk around before popping into the kitchen for a cup of tea. As he left, he gave me a cheque. I only looked at it after he had gone – it was for £150,000. Well in no uncertain way, God had once again said he would provide, and that gentleman became a consistent supporter.

"Ok Lord – how do we do it? That's a lot of money." We had quotations for rebuilding and that was at £15 per bird using the existing equipment totalling £360,000. At our monthly prayer meeting someone jokingly suggested we sponsor a hen for £15 and so via our church, newsletter and various customers, the message went out and the response was awesome. Over a two-year period we burnt the old sheds down and built new ones.

In 2001 when foot and mouth struck, our shop had to close but eggs could still go out wholesale on a disinfected lorry. The countryside came to a standstill and our sheep were destroyed in what was called 'the cull'.

In some ways it was a relief, as every day we had to go out and inspect them. I remember one day seeing a ewe limping and phoned the help line. He was obviously used to listening to weeping farmers and I explained the symptoms. He assured me we had not got foot and mouth, but it was still upsetting to see 200 healthy animals killed.

At that time we were working with the YOS on a project named the 'Restorative Justice Project'. This is where a young person would be found guilty in court but was too young to go to prison, so their sentence would be to come to us instead on a non-residential basis.

We had a steady flow of very nervous young people coming to us expecting to be punished in some way but they were all welcomed with arms open wide. Then off we went egg collecting or vegetable picking. We never asked why they were with us, that was up to them to tell us if they wanted to.

On one occasion I was collecting eggs with a lad and had to reprimand him. He was carrying a stack of fifteen dozen eggs and just threw them at me. I was ankle deep in broken eggs; he stood there expecting to be thrown out. (At some point Beryl and I had decided we would never ask anyone to leave, which was sorely tested at times). I said "John, why did you do that?" He was so shocked at my response that he burst into tears and we sat down and talked. He took his shirt off and showed me his back which was covered in dog bites where his dad had set the dog on him when he couldn't do his homework.

There were many similar stories to this one and each one was an opportunity to share the love of Jesus. However it was often preceded by an explosion of anger.

As part of my journey, I have noted that knowing my Jesus is not an easy way to go, I have a sure and certain knowledge that He is always with us. I have seen that when the going is rough those are the times people around us see the real Jesus, and we know He will never leave us or forsake us – we are not alone.

One example of this is a story about a diesel delivery. We had received the delivery; however the next day we discovered that it had been stolen. That was a lot of money and at coffee time as I was telling the lads I broke down and cried. Most of those lads had probably stolen at some time but had maybe never witnessed the effect it had on the person they had stolen from. It was a real eye opener for some of them.

Another occasion comes to mind from that year. We would sometimes purchase calves for the lads to rear. The calves arrive with a passport which we have to send in to ADAS to register them in our name. You are allowed ten days.

Dave had sent off five passports, but one had got delayed in the post, arriving a day late. We had a letter to say that the calf must be destroyed (unbelievable but true). I appealed as they were all posted together but unless I had proof of postage the calf would have to be destroyed.

That went on for a year, with the lads becoming very involved at prayer time. Then a neighbour phoned me. He knew of our problem and told me that one of his heifers had died during the night. He was suggesting that we swapped animals and ear tags so that I could phone ADAS and tell them that the illegal animal had died.

I shared this at coffee time and it seemed like a huge answer to prayer, but then I realised we were telling the lads it was ok to tell lies.

We have a huge responsibility to show integrity in everything we do. So I arranged for the calf to be destroyed and removed costing us £100!

During the foot and mouth epidemic it was clear how little the public knew about farming and their food. So when it was over, we decided to open the farm to the public.

At first it was just Saturdays, owing to fact that we had students Monday to Friday, but eventually we opened six days a week only closing on a Sunday. The students loved it. They enjoyed showing people around and answering questions which was another huge benefit to the educational value of Happy Hens.

Around this time I was contacted by Gordon Gatwood from the Rank Organisation, to come to a meeting at their head office at Stoneleigh, to look into the possibility of starting the National Care Farming Initiative (NCFI).

It had come to their attention that there were dozens of farms doing similar work to us with little support and so the NCFI was launched.

As Happy Hens was already well known, I became involved with various television and radio programmes. Our steering group was invited by Prince Charles to Highgrove. I was twice invited to Parliament and we also had several invites to Westminster and a full Question Time in Parliament. The local press printed lots of articles.

Our MP at the time was Mark Todd who was passionate about us and realised that we were a school, a youth offending service, and a commercial farm. Mark was also responsible within the Rank Organisation for my MBE. On 1st January 2011 we were officially told and Beryl and I took our eldest grandsons Jo and Nyle to Buckingham Palace to receive our 'gong'.

Our fame was spreading and we had a visitor from London. A Lord! He came at coffee time and was very impressed. We then went for a walk round the farm and I explained how angry hands became gentle hands when egg collecting. "When a new student arrives we get a lot of broken eggs" I explained "but usually by the end of the first day they could collect an egg without breaking it, no one wants egg all over themselves." Our visitor roared with laughter at the angry hands becoming gentle hands and it became our statement as it was the first of many life changing miracles that that young person would experience here.

As we opened up the farm to the public, we also started hosting school visits. Beryl and I went on a course about making the most of what we have as a farm. Beryl being Beryl went to town and with the help of our daughter Kelly, who had a diploma in Early Years Education, created the most amazing course for each age group and we quickly became very well known as the 'best school day out' in the area.

Buses started to arrive, and we could host from just a few up to ninety children a day. Our students enjoyed helping us which was good for them, and Happy Hens had added another string to their bow.

When the foot and mouth was over, farmers were deluged with paper work and forms to fill in. We had already signed up with the Lion scheme and RSPCA Freedom Food for the eggs and they too involved a lot of form filling and audits became the in thing. Each organisation had its own audit and no one seemed to have the common sense to pay one inspector to do them all.

On one particular day we had two - ADAS and the Lion Code of Practice. The RSPCA was a full day and in the beginning the inspector spent the whole day inspecting the hens and the range, but as forms appeared the RSPCA trip round the farm grew shorter and the day was spent in the office checking the paper work.

Needless to say, none of us were very clever in that way, so we got into plenty of trouble. The hens were brilliant but the paper work was not good.

Also in the 1990's we converted a small barn into a packing shed and shop. Dad and Elaine had moved into the barn and financed the next barn which a trust were completing, and a next door neighbour started to build a house in a field over the hedge from us.

One evening during a prayer meeting we went over to the neighbour's field. The concrete foundations had been laid that day and we all stood on that concrete and claimed the house for the Lord.

Before the house was finished, the neighbour fell out big time with our difficult neighbour down the drive and he left it unfinished. Little did we know at the time of that prayer meeting that two years later, dad would buy that house, 'The Paddocks', still unfinished, and give it to us. God can do more than we could ever ask for or imagine.

We still had a gang of YTS lads with us who had been a great help building the foundations for the chicken sheds and they now moved on to completing 'The Paddocks'.

It took two years before we could move in and allow the trust to have the farmhouse and the first barn (they were already using the second barn

The egg business was booming and the little shop was busy. We moved the shop down to The Paddocks alongside a small tea-room introducing vegetables from South Derbyshire Growers, and pickles and jams from Beryl.

We were also on BBC TV 'Songs of Praise' as our fame of working with impossible youngsters had spread. On the programme the then head of YOS said on TV that the reoffending rate for that age group was 80% but no one who had come to 'Highfields Happy Hens' had reoffended. WOW!! What a statistic.

Shortly after that however a lad came to us very pale and thin and stinking of wee. We gave him breakfast every day before we started work. He didn't want to leave at the end of his sentence. So shortly after he left we had a call from YOS that he had reoffended and demanded to come back to 'Highfields Happy Hens'. This was a bit embarrassing but a huge compliment.

He had not been to school for three years and so we met with the head of the school and agreed that he should come to us as school rather than keep reoffending.

Well after one term he was going into college and invited Beryl and I to his parents evening. Upon leaving college he was employed straight away.

That's My Jesus. Who said many years ago that even God could not find them a job? And yet God proved me wrong!

We met with the education authority again and they asked "How did we do that? Did we enjoy it?" Yes definitely!!

We had lots of lads similar to him and so our life changed dramatically. We were taking up to nine young people a day and we were being paid quite well. Our reputation for getting youngsters back to school was awesome.

Common sense came into play. Why wait till the youngster had been excluded? Why not let them have one or two days at 'Highfields' and stay at school? That reduced the number being excluded and had a much better educational outcome.

At one time we had been involved with an OFSTED inspection. His report was one paragraph –

"What can I say? These are children no one else will have." Well, if you ask, Jesus will give you a love for the unlovable and believe me it is exciting to see broken lives turn around.

Roger with his hens 2014

Roger and Beryl...Both smiling at the same time!!

—1952 Horse Guards Parade, London Roger 10 years old with a catapult in his pocket!!

59 years later!!

Same place—Roger with his MBE and a Bible in his pocket!

I Want You to Meet My Jesus

Chapter 24

Coffee Time

Since the beginning of working with young people we always had a coffee break at 10.30am. This always ended with a short time of prayer which was a great and varied experience, but in the main it was mostly accepted with a sense of respect and peace. On one occasion a social worker had come to see how two of his lads were getting on. He stayed for coffee and after prayer time I looked up to see he was crying as his two 'impossible' lads were sitting quietly with their hands together and their eyes shut.

Another memorable coffee time experience was with a lad who was with us who had worse than the usual bad language. We did put up with bad language as it was the language of their home, school and even television but we did let them know we didn't like it. While we were working with this boy, he would *"f'in"* this and *"f'in"* that and I simply said, "You don't need to use that language." A few days later we had a new lad in and at coffee time he was swearing away when my bad language friend went up to him and told him "They don't like that kind of language here mate!" Well what a silent victory!

We made a point of asking visitors to come at coffee time as it was a good time to meet staff and students, MPs, social workers, and teachers. Most were very impressed but on one occasion a teacher asked me "do you have to do that?" referring to the prayer time, I explained that praying was the backbone of all we do.

In the early days of this arrangement, there were no rules, just to keep them happy and out of trouble. But the government had begun to realise that more and more young people were being educated out of school and so should be offered a formal education. This was a good idea in theory but bureaucracy at its worst. We were good at emotional healing and getting kids back to school but now we had to include formal education which was of course precisely what had been causing the problem.

Our schools were devastated as none of our staff were 'qualified' and we were told we could not take any more students from September. Then our faithful lady from the Local Education Authority said, "You are already doing these things with the eggs, veg, money and shop". All we needed to do was record it. That solved our problem and we were off again, so much so that at the end of the first term we were held up as a shining example, but it was the beginning of our nightmare and eventually our undoing.

PAPERWORK!

Written in October 2010 -

"This has been a real turning point for me and I feel I should record it in detail. A project that looks after youngsters excluded, or in danger of being excluded from school. We have grown and become more complex, particularly as a result of endless legislation and paperwork both for the farm and education. To cover this our team has grown with 'department managers' being needed to take the pressure off Beryl and me.

That had resulted in handing over responsibilities and accepting new ways of doing things. As a team we meet together to pray each day and we know we are available to each other at any time for support and prayer."

As this had happened I in particular had become more of an administrator which I struggled with. I had less to do with the students which I found very hard as that was my vision, and what I enjoyed most. It had been so essential to the smooth running of the project, as in November 2009 I had a replacement knee fitted and then shortly after that I was diagnosed with prostate cancer and started to receive radiotherapy. Both these things removed me from the working team completely although I was able to go out to the morning staff/prayer meeting. I became very tired and unable to cope and everything started getting on top of me.

During that time I was not sleeping well so most nights I got up and read my Bible from 1am until 4am. My new knee would not get comfortable and the radiotherapy was burning my groin. Psalm 20 was my favourite but I read several books completely and picked up a whole lot of memorised scripture verses. Unfortunately, although I was quoting them, I ceased to believe them. I prayed a lot but stopped expecting my prayers to be answered.

When in July I had my blood test results to say my cancer was gone "Thank you Jesus," we decided to go on the holiday of a lifetime. I had saved a year and a half of my state pension and off we went to the Maldives. It rained every day which was bad enough but two days before coming home Beryl slipped and damaged her back. I was then in a state of panic. We were on an island with no medical help and the only way off was a forty five minute bumpy sea plane ride.

We prayed. Beryl was sure she was only bruised so we set off for home. The tour operator arranged for us to see a doctor at Male airport who dosed Beryl up with pain killers and off we went on a fifteen hour flight, towards the end of which my bottom was aching quite badly. I asked Beryl how she was and she told me she was ok. When we arrived back home I took her to A&E to discover her coccyx was broken and displaced. How did we make it home? Not without a miracle as she could not even sit in the car seat comfortably for weeks after that.

As I was slipping into a bad state spiritually, I started to read a book that had been in our bedroom for ages. It had been given to me by a dear friend who runs a healing room in Norwich. 'Preparing the Way' was about the reopening of the healing rooms in Spokane, America and as I read something started to spark in me. Why had I stopped believing in prayer when others consistently believed in miracles as did we when we first came to the Lord?

The end of that week, Friday 8th October, I could not sleep, nor could I pray quietly so I went into the spare room. I went to sleep and then woke with what felt like a heavy, horrible body on top of me. I could not breathe or move my arms, and a smell of sulphur. In panic I called out for Beryl to help me. The bedroom door opened and someone came in, knelt by my bed, and laid a hand on me. The horrible weight left me and I laid there stiff and terrified. After a while I reached out to touch the person thinking it was Beryl but there was no-one there and the bedroom door was closed. Later Beryl told me it was not her, so I was convinced that the devil had been holding me down and that Jesus had come and released me.

Saturday I was full of mixed emotions, scared of what had happened and yet knowing that God was calling me back. Sunday, I wrote some notes, determined to ask the church to stand with me in a personal mission to be re-filled by the Holy Spirit. I had to confess I had stopped believing in prayer, that although the project on the farm was growing and young lives were being changed all I could see was a chicken farm with a mountain of debt. I needed to be released from the shame of that and once again experience the joy that God wanted me to have; but also to start believing in prayer as well as praying more and to give Gideon Bibles to all the people I met in the course of my work.

Chapter 25

I Let Myself Down

"Monday I really let myself down and probably got as close as I will ever get to having another nervous breakdown. Finances have always been a problem to me (needless to say God has always provided but my lack of faith let me down). We had a small tractor that we did not use much so I asked the team if it was ok for me to sell it. I phoned the dealer expecting £5,000 but he offered me £7,000 – wow "Thank you Jesus." I shared this at coffee time but remembered that it had been purchased with a grant in 2003. I told Dave and we felt that after all this time they would have forgotten, but my new awakened spirit was not happy.

I began looking through a seven-year-old file not wanting to find anything. But then there it was - the tractor could not be sold without their permission. Sadly, I went to pieces – sell it or tell them and risk losing £7,000. I quite simply did not want to do things God's way. I was hysterical.

I know it sounds daft now but £7,000 was a lot of money. Beryl came rushing in to find out what the fuss was about. She texted everyone on the farm "Roger's lost it." Dave came rushing in to pray for me but he and Beryl both agreed that we had no alternative but to contact the grant people.

I sat there for a while knowing I had no option. I phoned all the numbers on the seven-year-old correspondence; however, they were all discontinued. Surely I had done my best and it was now ok to sell it? But my spirit was still not at ease, so I wrote to the address I had found and posted the letter first class.

The next day giants began to fall and at 4pm we had an email. The grant body had closed down leaving one person in charge, congratulating us on the work we were doing and giving us permission to sell. WOW! "Thank you Jesus."

Just another lesson learned – God wants things done properly – a sleeping spirit will not give you much hassle, but an awakened spirit will lead you in the clearest and best way with God's Blessing. Other giants fell that week too. I began praying for people in a more natural and spontaneous way and needed to restock with Gideon Bibles."

10ᵗʰ October 2010 - A prophetic word received

"I saw a pile of muck in a farm yard. Next to it was a muck spreader and tractor — the muck spreader was being loaded ready to go to the field. I saw the field and the muck spreader had just started. Once the muck is spread the field is left fallow until the muck has been absorbed.

I feel that the Lord is saying to you and Beryl that He wants you both to be as the meadow, lying fallow; absorb the goodness that the Lord is putting in to you both and He will tell you when the ground can be prepared to do what He requires of it.

Two things Roger, the Lord has since been saying to me that you should note the time and date - the reason I am saying this is because after the muck has been carted away it leaves an impression on the ground to remind you of His providence.

The second thing, which is just a feeling that I have, is that as the muck heap diminishes so will Beryl's pain and the healing is in place."

11ᵗʰ October 2010 - Vision received at Sunday morning service

"While we were praying for Roger and Beryl I could see a marathon race taking place; the runners were dressed in colourful t-shirts and shorts. Roger and Beryl were encouraging people to join them in the race and people began to follow on behind as the race progressed. As I

watched I could see Roger and Beryl suffer physical ailments which at first began to slow them down as they tried to keep running. Eventually they were unable to run so had to sit out the race as spectators watching from the side-lines as the runners ran past. I could sense this was not an easy thing to do as they were used to leading from the front. The word I sensed that came from God was REST in Him and wait for your bodies to be healed and restored."

30th October 2010 -

"Occasionally people have told us we are wasting our time, that we are not doing these kids any good, that we are doing it all wrong. It is so easy to reject that kind of talk. Yes it hurts and even makes you feel like giving up, but we have to ask God if there is any truth in these comments, is there anything He wants to say to us through them?

This week it has happened again – "Lord please show us if we are wrong or confirm what we are doing is your will." In a few minutes we are off to the Lake District for a good sleep but just before leaving a young man came to the door – his partner has come to wander round the farm – why?

She had been with us as a teenager. She is now twenty five years old with only a few months to live as cancer is spreading through her. She remembered she had felt good at 'Highfields' and came for a walk round. He gave me a cheque for £1,150 to plant a tree and towards the wind turbine. I had to go out and find her, to pray with her and to give her a Gideon Bible. Surely she is too young to die and she came back here to find peace.

What more confirmation do we need ? God is so good."

As I write in 2022 this same woman is now married with 2 children. We have no idea how many lives have been changed by the love and peace of Jesus in this place.

I say this was the beginning of the end as like farming, the paperwork became more important than the students. We were still getting stunning results and life transformations but our paperwork was rubbish – Health & Safety, risk assessments, daily reports; we had to have at least two first aiders and a student safeguarding officer. All of a sudden it was all going wrong and we were constantly in trouble.

On one occasion we had a fifteen-year-old girl, very pregnant and she was smoking. I put my hand on her shoulder and said, "You're not doing your baby any good." She got quite upset and the next day I had to attend a disciplinary meeting. After the meeting, the lady who headed the meeting came to me and apologised and said she would have done the same thing.

Our world was falling apart and we suspected a strong anti-Christian motive, as the list of our apparent failures grew despite our incredible record with the youngsters. However in the end we lost our contract worth £75,000 a year.

I am not sure where obedience comes into this. We had a wonderful faithful staff and no students. Happy Hens was going downhill as the supermarkets had driven the price of eggs down so that, as so often happens in farming, they priced the small producers out of the market.

Our hope and prayer now was that God would still send us youngsters we could help which He did, but there had been a recession and youngsters were falling through the net with no support. Unfortunately, our supporters of long ago had got older, moved, or died. We lost a lot of our egg agents and we began borrowing money. Was that the mistake?

We built a huge wind turbine which did provide an income but we were getting deeper into debt and I began to get into trouble with the bank with no clear way out.

Chapter 26

We're in Trouble

At last we had to admit we were in trouble so my faithful prayer partner Alan, came with me to visit the head of Derby City Mission and he told us of a trust looking to start a Christian education base for young offenders stating that Highfields would be perfect. That evening a trustee phoned us in high excitement. There followed some very professional, structured meetings with a chairman and secretary. I was given a date to retire and be off the farm and a service was organised in Derby Cathedral.

It was the Trust's birthday party and an introduction to their plans for Highfields. There was wine and cake and forms to fill in to sponsor the project. A lot of money was raised that night. All of our staff together with a lot of other interested people attended and it sounded so incredible. All of our staff had been through a proper interview and offered a job.

After some weeks things went quiet, meetings were getting fewer, it was approaching our retirement date and as we had to move the Trust had agreed to provide us with a suitable home. At a memorably awful meeting we were told we would have to rent a house which was definitely not the plan and then we got an email to say they were pulling out. The farm was a mess as we had been told not to maintain anything as it was all going to be rebuilt.

What can I say? There were weeks of shocked silence but we had to get our heads round it, tidy the place up and put it up for sale.

7th August 2016 - A word from a lady at church

"The Lord has asked me to tell you He has given you two keys; the keys are Praise and Thanksgiving (thankfulness). These keys if you use them will release the power of God that will set you free. He asked me to remind you of when Paul and Silas were in prison – how instead of dwelling on their circumstances they focused on praising the Lord. As they did the Power of God was released setting them free from captivity and many were saved as a result.

The Lord knows your need and your contrite heart; He has plans for you plans to prosper and to give you hope."

(There are some big gaps in my diary at this time)

God reminded me of a story that helps me in times of doubt, fear or worry:-

A small child from a Christian family was asked by her teacher "Where is Jesus now?" After some thought the child answered, "In my heart." Then the teacher asked, "What will you do if Satan comes knocking on the door of your heart?" After further thought she replied, "I would ask Jesus to open the door."

I find fear is a constant problem and I have this picture that I am in a room or a field with Jesus. There is a knock on the door. Satan bends down and looks through the key hole and sees no one coming towards the door. He knows he has got me. But no! That's not the way it should be! What I have learnt over recent months. Has really helped.

Back to the same situation. There's the knock on the door. I say, "Jesus Jesus."

"What do you want me to do for you my child?"

"Jesus will you open the door?"

"Yes my child, you just sit there and trust Me, I will go and deal with your enemy."

Satan bends down to look through the key hole and sees the Son of God coming towards the door and he is off like a shot. Jesus opens the door and Satan has gone.

"My child" He says to me *"You have won the victory".*

I reply, "No you won the victory."

"No my child you won the victory."

"But Lord I did not do anything, just sat still and trusted you".

"Yes my child that is the way you and I are going to fight your battles in future."

4th June 2017 - Another word for us at church

"What God gave me: two enormous doors - one was rusty and one was golden. What the Lord is saying is God has seen you patiently waiting. In that time the door has gone rusty. In that time God has seen the patience. What God is saying is that the golden door has opened for you, and only you and God can open it. God is saying that He will take you through this door to new opportunities that are waiting for you – the time is right now for you to go through the golden gate."

4th September 2017 – "I have lost count of the times I have decided to write my story. I hope that I have kept enough notes, although some false starts will have got lost in old computers, maybe one day to be discovered and added in. I get so far and then wonder "Who will want to read my story anyway?" But then I know that millions will be searching for Jesus, maybe without realising it – looking for something to believe in but not sure what. Even now as I look at the screen my mind goes blank and I want to switch off. The phone rings, life goes on. But I feel it is time to start putting it all together and to try to record my search for something to believe in - how I spent most of my young life until I was forty years old knowing there was 'something'.

Until that age I was in a Christian family and school, then just a church member, until on one of my bad days I remembered the comment "My God is alive sorry to hear about yours." I was totally insulted, but thankfully I looked at him and then at me and knew what he meant. My God was not alive, He was in a rundown building and a very boring book, the Bible.

That's when Beryl and I started searching and listening. We were beginning to witness prayers being answered, people being healed. God is very gentle and moves one step at a time; He is not slow but moves at our speed. Slowly the Bible became alive as we met the Author. But still there was something missing and we were introduced to the existence of the Holy Spirit and the need to be born again. We were so excited. Our new life bursting with a new relationship with Jesus, who was about to take over our lives in the most positive and fantastic way – we had discovered and accepted the 'something else'.

Our times at Hollybush Farm with Jim Wilkinson, and his wife Cynthia, introducing us to the Holy Spirit. We were prayed for many times and often drove up to their Friday evening service with a van full of youngsters. On one particular occasion I found myself flat on my back. It is difficult to find words; for this experience. I could hear what was going on around me; my mind seemed to be in another place; utterly peaceful (slain in the Spirit). I felt someone hold my hand who said that God would give me healing hands.

Since then I have kept claiming that wonderful miracle, but then sitting here writing this, I know that dozens of young people have passed through 'Highfields' and have been emotionally healed. It would seem that I have been asking for something that God had already given me years ago. I wonder how many other things God has given us that we have not acknowledged?"

Chapter 27

The Prayer of Jabez

"Oh that you would bless me and enlarge my territory! Let your hand be with me and keep me from harm so that I will be free from pain." And God answered his request. 1Chronicles 4:10 (NIV)

Excerpts from my diary:-

1ˢᵗ October 2018 - The lead up to this bit is in my sort of diary but it involves The Prayer of Jabez and the follow up "You were born for this". A lot I didn't agree with as it seemed to make prayer more complicated, but it did emphasise hearing God's voice.

"Ok – the past two days have been like pages out of a book, the kind of stuff you think "Why doesn't that happen to me?" It has been about learning to trust in apparently hopeless situations and learning to listen."

2ⁿᵈ October 2018 - "We are both emotionally exhausted; spiritually we are ok but getting a bit cross with God. There is a trip booked in for today and when Beryl looked at the diary it was for seventy five children. By 9am Ashley was not in and we knew James would be late so Mick rushed off to start collecting the eggs. I panicked. Needless to say Ashley appeared, then James and Mick helped us with what turned out to be a lovely group split into three groups – that doesn't sound much of a miracle but imagine seventy two children and 10,000 eggs to collect.

Tuesday evening prayer meeting – I have been struggling as we seem to have spent three years since the Trust pulled out, not really wanting to be here, and battling to keep the place and vision going – fantastic evening full of worship and prayer. I saw a lady limping as she left and said we cannot leave a prayer meeting without praying for her. We did all the right things but she was still limping – will we ever know what God wants to do?!"

(The next bit is too long to record without names) – Suffice it to say that with the Estate Agent's agreement we accepted an offer for the farm with a delayed payment. Six months later we had an instant cash offer. The Estate Agent agreed to contact the first offer and they agreed that if it was a cash offer they would withdraw – many months later the cash offer withdrew too!! And the first offer was no longer interested!!!"

3rd October 2018 - 'Quite distressed this morning and very prayerful! It's the Brailsford Ploughing Match with the Gideons.

We have a student who can be very violent. We knew that last weekend he had put his granddad in hospital and ended up being arrested. He had been very peaceful on Monday but today he was agitated and annoying the staff. I was sure there was going to be a fight and decided I could not go to the ploughing match. Mick took the lad out to B&Q. I then went to the garage for petrol. How did this happen? I paid for the fuel and then said to the lady "Can I give you a present?" "Yes" she hesitantly replied. "Can I give you my Bible?" I asked (I always have one in my pocket). She took it and smiled. I squeezed her hand and left. I might not have been at the ploughing match but I can still give a Bible!!

A short while later our daughter Kelly phoned with a message from her friend at the garage. "Your dad has just been in – isn't he a sweetie – he gave me his Bible. How did he know I was struggling?" Wow, Praise God! I cried. Beryl asked me why I was crying to which I replied, "I think I am learning to hear God's voice".

Brailsford Ploughing Match. - It's strange, I love giving Bibles away and I love being involved with young people, but in that situation I felt intrusive walking up to strangers asking if they would like a Bible. I was told we could only give out Bibles on our patch which seemed to make it even more threatening as there were five of us. I rebelliously wandered off, bumped into people I knew and kept having to go back to the tent for more Bibles.

This morning I had dealt with a potentially threatening situation and felt comfortable with that. I guess the other Gideons would have felt uncomfortable but here they were chatting away with strangers and me feeling very uncomfortable."

5ᵗʰ October 2018 - "I must keep writing as things happen. We had a disabled group with us today. One of the teachers was on her phone and as she walked towards us another teacher said, "Was that the doctor?" "Yes." came her reply "Are you ok?" What an opportunity to give her a Bible or a nudge from God. I did not want to embarrass her and did not see her on her own so went home thinking that I had misheard, but I was unsettled so said to God "I will walk to the party room and if she is somewhere on her own I will deliver a Bible to her." Then out she came all alone walking towards the tea-room. "Thank you Lord" – delivery completed.

Sometime later the head teacher came to Beryl - "Roger gave a member of staff a Bible, and she said to me How did he know?"

6th October 2018 - "Last night I was a bit spiritually overwhelmed. "What are you saying to me Lord?" "*Learn to hear My voice.*" Came the reply. So I started to read the next chapter of "You were born for This" It was about helping people who need to forgive. That was a bit much for me to cope with so I closed the book and read a novel. Well guess what. I was due to meet an old friend for lunch. During the conversation we talked about family. He has a brother he has not seen for over forty years who split the family. So I asked if we could try to find him and if he needed to, forgive him. Needless to say I also had a lot of forgiving to do.

God is responding to me as each day I now pray "Lord lead me to someone who needs a miracle". To be honest it's quite frightening but also very exciting. Be careful of what you pray for! That does not mean stop praying but choose to follow up that prayer with "Here I am, Lord use me" and then EXPECT God to lead you to a person who needs what you have got."

4th November 2018 - "It's been a long time since I wrote anything here or in my 'sort of' diary.

It's been a long painful journey trying to sell the farm. It's four years ago since the Trust gave me a retirement date and since then there have been a lot of interested people. When they see our accounts and realise you cannot make money out of looking after broken people they back off and once again leave us dejected and depressed. Recently we have come to realise that God is taking us on a journey, preparing us for His future plans. Four years ago we were not mentally prepared for letting this place go, and each time someone nearly buys it we get a bit closer, but we have struggled in every way and learnt a lot.

When we are down and depressed we feel sorry for ourselves and maybe even angry with God. (He can cope with that). The Prayer of Jabez changed my thinking. "Oh Lord that you would Bless ME indeed, put your hand upon me and expand my ministry (territory)." We found it hard to pray that prayer because we did not want to expand our territory, we were trying to sell it. But then in Bruce Wilkinson's book he changes the word to ministry "Oh Lord Bless me so much that I overflow and long to Bless someone." I changed from a stagnant puddle to a life changing stream. Although tired, fed up, frustrated I can get up in the morning and beg God to give me someone to bless today(or more than one) and even allow me to be a channel for a miracle.

"Help me to learn to hear Your voice and overcome my fear of failure." Also I feel God is telling us to let the past go, to put down our dreams, (it has been my dream to have a farm and I have had one for fifty years), to let go of our life's work in Happy Hens, the shop, and the tea-room, and let go of our ministry with broken young people, which doesn't seem to make sense. Who will look after them? They are God's children and the little hen sheds are not economic. Is it possible we are near the end of a very painful pruning process preparing us for the time ahead and a new larger ministry? Can we trust Him to sell the farm now?

"So many awful things have happened recently Lord, we cannot take any more." I know the Bible says he will not give us more than we can bear but we have reached our limit. Getting out of bed for another day is a struggle, working out how to pay for all the things that are going wrong, with the massive drop in egg production, and the drop in egg price and the increase in feed cost. I then set fire to the tractor twice by putting the jump leads on the wrong way leaving me feeling embarrassed and ashamed. How could I make the same mistake twice? The turbine has broken – need I go on? But then I get a voice in my left ear as my right hearing aid was broken, *"Trust me Rog"* - it sounds so real. I am learning to hear His voice. He knows my weakest point - finance or lack of it - and He is teaching me to trust Him at my weakest point.

I must not run or allow depression and fear to come back and so I pray "Lord give me someone to bless today. Help me to make a difference in someone's life today. Help me to be still and abide with you, not in desperation but in love as spending time with a friend."

20th November 2018 -The story of the little red oil can.

So even though it was four years ago that we were told it was time to retire, there have been a lot of nearly-answers to massive prayers. Each time with a new lesson we needed to learn about hearing God's voice, and His plans for the future of the farm and our future ministry.

However through that period of waiting and big prayers not apparently being answered God has blessed us each day in a very small personal way. Something happened each day that at that moment was so important that it nearly pushed us over the edge, yet when repeated sounds so unimportant in the grand scheme of things. That is our Jesus. He cares so much for us and understands the small details.

On this particular day I got the van out to take Hayden to football. A very important granddad thing, unfortunately the sliding side door would not close properly. I needed an oil can but couldn't find one. I searched in the obvious places and was getting very stressed, I asked Beryl if she knew where I could find an oil can. Needless to say the last person to ask. "Yes, top shelf of my cupboard" and sure enough there was a little red oil can with oil in it.

I need to explain Beryl's very special cupboard. Her dad, Stanley was a very lovely practical guy and must be the only dad in the world to give his daughter spanners and other useful things. It was a bit of a joke with our children. Beryl had this cupboard filling up with stuff that occasionally was useful and on this occasion it literally saved my day. A rather strange present given on Sunday tea time many years ago just lying there waiting for that special day. There is a sermon there in that how often have we given or said something that appears to have no meaning or impact that will lay unused until that very special day? I often think that about our students.

They arrive as rebellious angry youngsters and leave transformed with seeds sown that one day will germinate. A newspaper reporter once asked me "What is your success rate?" I knew what he meant but I replied, "One hundred percent" and explained that every student that passed through here had had a seed planted in them.

Every day a little something blesses us and gives us the strength to handle the day. God has other ways of dealing with us. I have had a really low week spiritually "Lord I cannot take any more, please release me." A couple of days ago I went to Tesco with Beryl. I was glumly pushing the trolley when suddenly I thought "I should not feel like this, please God let me bless someone." Almost immediately I saw a frail old lady with her arm in a sling and pushing a trolley with one hand. "Have you hurt yourself?" I asked her "Yes I fell over," came the reply. "Oh dear" I said and I walked off. I felt God say, *"I want to heal her"* "Oh no not in the middle of Tesco" but then I said, "Ok if I see her again," and sure enough as I changed aisles there she was. I couldn't avoid her so I went up to her and said, "Hallo it's me again." Needless to say she looked a bit apprehensive and confused. "I believe God wants to heal your arm; can I pray for you?" I asked "Well that would be nice" was the reply. So, there in the middle of a busy Tesco I laid hands on her and prayed for healing, then gave her my little Bible. "That was lovely thank you." She said. I never saw her again.

In those few moments God had brought me back to basics. There were so many big things in my life over which I had no control and only God can deal with, but in my despair I had forgotten the real reason for my life. I would love to have been a fly on the wall when that lady got home. "You are not going to believe this a man came up to me in Tesco and prayed for my arm and gave me a Bible."

Chapter 28

When You're Down

When you feel really down, depressed, or distressed.

I have to admit that several times I have had depression. At one point several years ago I was off work and 'on the pills' for 6 months, deeply ashamed that Christians should not feel like that. I have been on the pills a time or two since then but discovered praying the 'Prayer of Jabez' ("Oh Lord that you would bless me indeed" but one step further, that I would overflow, and "Give me someone to bless.")

It is quite easy to be overwhelmed by circumstances, finances, health, family and to keep facing them is not always the best option. I make a bad decision to turn my back on it all, go in the bedroom, draw the curtains, lie on the bed, and just feel awful, but I know that the longer I lay there the worse I will feel. That seems like the only option but as soon as I ask God to bless me and ask him to give me someone to bless then the clouds begin to lift. Getting off the bed and out of the door is the first hurdle, but there is a spiritual strength and sure enough God WILL give you someone to bless. It can be quite a major situation with a stranger or simply to ask Beryl if she has had a good day, but it takes me away from the fear of the situation. Sadly, it can happen all over again, the next day and the next, but the positive is the blessing that God loves to give you. He loves it, even more, when you pass it on.

This is a massive step towards the reason for me writing this book. I am finding more of Jesus and learning that He is with me all the time. It has to be my act of will to say, "Lord I can't handle this on my own." He longs to bless us, particularly in the dark times. At those times He can bring light, rest, heal, and deliver us. The Bible tells us He will never ask from us more than we can cope with. I often feel that He has gone too far, that I just cannot cope, but then He gives me that extra strength.

There are reasons for depression, feeling that God is a long way away or have we done something wrong or sinful? Do not beat yourself up! Our spirit will give us the answer to that and if we know we are doing something wrong then there is no dodging it. Put it right and confess it. For me I have a problem from November onwards and the shorter days. My doctor calls them my sunshine pills, but over the years I have noticed that my ability to cope mentally has dropped. Still I fight against it and try to pray it away. I gave in two days ago and took the pills and feel much better.

There is a lovely example in the Bible of Elijah that helps me. He has just seen the most amazing turn around with God bringing fire from heaven. But then he hears a word from Jezebel and he runs over one hundred miles, lies down, and tells God he wants to die. Facing fear of death and persecution he falls into a depression. He says to himself "I am useless, I have failed, I want to die." Elijah went from victory to wanting to die! How did that happen? Once you start running all sorts of terrible things enter your mind. Fight them or run? I have found the best way to deal with them is to turn to my Jesus.

I can look back over my life and remember the depression but for the life of me I cannot remember what the problem was!!

As I write this the farm has been for sale for a long time; everyone is telling us to let go but each day the farm has to operate, students have to be cared for and blessed. There have been several close-to-sold situations and just now an almost definite. We had hoped that the church would buy it and our amazing ministry would continue. Two years ago our pastor and our group of friends warned us that it was destroying us physically and mentally so we must let go and allow anyone who had the money to buy it. Yesterday (26.11.18) I went back on the pills. I was overwhelmed and sure that God really did want the ministry to continue; after all it is Holy ground. Yes I still go into my bedroom and feel awful for a while, knowing that He will never leave me or forsake me but also knowing that the sooner I pray the "Jabez Prayer" the sooner I will feel better. Night Shelter is just starting for another winter so I will have lots of opportunities to be a blessing. But also opportunities to say I just can't cope!!!

Another black morning - "Oh Lord that you would bless me indeed and let me be a blessing." And lo and behold He has done it again. We rent the grassland to a mega shepherd who has sheep all over the country. He is a really nice man and a good stock man. Last week thirty of his ewes drowned in the brook at the bottom of our farm. Almost certainly a dog had frightened them. I phoned him but he was in hospital with a kidney infection, pneumonia and the antibiotics had upset his diabetes. He was coming out of hospital and he and his son came for the bodies. I assured him we would pray for him. Well yesterday there were three more in the brook and I just could not begin to imagine how it was all affecting him.

Another black morning - "Oh Lord that you would bless me indeed and let me be a blessing."

The doorbell rang and there was my mega sheep man looking really ill. I threw my arms around him and blessed him then gave him a Bible. If it hadn't been such a sad situation it would have been funny, his face was a picture of shock but also helplessness. He is a big friendly guy and certainly not used to being hugged. God had sent me someone to bless. I went back in the house, shut the door, and cried, again remembering why we are Christians and how God will use us if we are willing. I want him to meet my Jesus!!

15th December 2018 - I must write today as I believe a penny has dropped, God is so patient. It can take many years for us to understand what has been staring us in the face for years. I have a book 'A – Z of Happiness', and every night when I switch the light out I recite it to myself as I go to sleep.

A is for attitude!!! Yes it's the first letter and I recite it every night but today I understand what it means.

The farm and project has been for sale for several years. Suffice it to say for every potential buyer who comes along we have to get our head round a different method of payment, splitting the farm up, a completely different use for the farm. Just as we feel we are being obedient to the process of passing it on that person pulls out and a new one turns up with completely different ideas, and

215

we have to pray for patience and wisdom all over again.

Needless to say our attitude has, to say the least, not been good. We have even got cross and frustrated with God (He can cope with that) but each new person who comes along takes us down a different apparent dead end. I say apparent because that did not happen. But we did learn something. There is a jigsaw puzzle beginning to take place.

In many ways it has been an awful week but over the years we can truthfully say that everyday Jesus has touched us, and in a very real way shown us He is right beside us, and that His world is so much bigger than ours. Well my prayer had been answered.

Three days later he (the mega sheep man) passed the canteen, saw us, and again he looked like he was going to die. No need to ask him how he felt. So without thinking I dragged him into a chair between Alan and me and said, "We are going to lay hands on this guy" and that's what we did. There was a real feeling in the air. I phoned him a few days later to find out how he was and he said he was completely healed! This all started with my anguished cry for an angel. God had wanted to heal him and needed me to deliver it. **A is for attitude**. I could have just laid on the bed and cried.

Somewhere I have read that God doesn't do miracles, He does them through us! Could that be why we do not see enough miracles today?

In that same week, the turbine had been broken for six weeks and the company dealing with it were not answering the phone. I was beginning to think they had gone bust and our turbine was in bits all over the field. Sam from Betel came in for prayers and coffee and we discussed this before praying about it. Then the phone rang which I answered on loudspeaker. It was someone from the turbine company, who was full of apologies. This was a massive answer to prayer, for me, another miracle, heard by everyone present. Sam then came into the house and we had a long chat about the future of the farm.

Financially we are in a big mess and I had been trying to get hold of the bank to increase our overdraft, but I felt God was saying *"You must not be afraid to share your pain."* So my fingers wrote a newsletter. My dyslexia causes me to struggle with writing in the natural, but I know when God wants to write something He uses my fingers.

Some time ago I was speaking at a meeting in Matlock and on the way home I felt God was saying *"Your debts will be paid before the farm is sold."* Since then everything seemed to go in the opposite direction, when this happens we have to stand on God's promises. When we were baptised people reminded us that Jesus went into the wilderness for forty days after He was baptised. So He too understands the wilderness times in our lives.

Friday of that week I took Beryl out for a meal. Needless to say we spent the evening moaning and trying to work out what was happening to us, and then I asked her a question "Do we really believe God has got a plan?" "Yes." "Do we really believe God wants to bless us?" "Yes," and then it dawned on me A is for attitude!!!! In the Bible it often says to be full of joy at all times and that has seemed impossible for me. Now we know what that means. This morning I reminded us both, and as usual prayed that God would let me bless someone today, but also remind me that A is for attitude.

I feel in my heart that this is the most important message of the whole book:-

Example:-"I am dreading this evening – don't be surprised if this evening is awful"

Or "I am not looking forward to this evening but it will still be good."

A is for attitude!

20th December 2018 - Today I do not want to write anything and in fact I don't want to remember anything that has happened over the past few days or weeks, but I am also conscious that the reader needs to know something of the struggles we have had. My memory is awful yet I know good things have happened but when we are in the valley it is too easy to let the blackness envelop us and we can get overwhelmed with self-pity. We need to remind ourselves to focus on God's Love for us and that Jesus is with us all the time, He will never leave us or forsake us. He always has a plan.

By my bed is a stack of good books 'When Heaven is Silent', 'Heaven on Mute', 'I shouldn't feel like this' and many more – it is good to know that others (even '*big*' people) have gone through the valley. In the end it is down to me and God.

Almost every source of finance had being cut off. A long time ago our student income was cut dramatically, as we got lost in paperwork, risk assessments, Health &Safety and schools were short of money. But we kept our staff/team in the certain knowledge that we had so much to offer, and yes students did come who had no financial support as well as a few who did. However all along my 'problem' has been focussing on what I love to do – **working with broken lives**. That is what I wanted to do and where I was gifted to be able to help. All the other duties and jobs were hard for me to manage, for instance the chickens were a constant problem but essential to our ministry in providing work for **'angry hands'.**

When the egg production dropped and the turbine broke for several weeks all seemed lost. The turbine people came and took it to bits, with some of the parts taken away. They gave me several dates to come back, but with their own problems there was quite a delay. I kept telling them we would pray for them and blessed them in all my emails. I wonder if they have other let-down customers that are swearing and cussing, and yet I want them to know God's love through my attitude.

This is possibly costing us potentially £100 a day in lost income, but God keeps reminding me that we must depend on Him to provide and our attitude to those we deal with is what we are all about. It's easy to praise and worship when the going is good and much harder when things seem to go wrong, or in worldly terms just plain awful.

The bank begrudgingly agreed to lend us more money and I wrote a heart-breaking newsletter to our key supporters. As you can guess I am not very good at standing still while He fights my battles or in 'being still and knowing that He is God'. I feel I must be doing something and that is my undoing because I know that means I am not trusting Him. My excuse is that I am a practical guy and decisions must be made. Finance is my big weakness, and so I spend all my time worrying and feeling sure I must do something.

One of the authors I have read had been through terrible times and decided to get up early and spend one and a half hours with the Lord and His word every morning. How do you do that? But I was resolved, so one morning, I was up, did my exercises and then lay on my face on the lounge floor, struggling to worship. Next time I looked at my watch it was two hours later. I don't think I went to sleep but I don't think I worshipped for two hours either. Then the newsletters arrived from the printers. This was my big plan to ask for help.

G is for generosity - I know that I will always feel better if I bless someone with my time or a gift so I phoned Betel to see if they could use our biggest turkey. Someone had given us £50 to pay for it. They said they had been given enough turkeys and asked if they could collect one after Christmas. I got talking to Karen and told her of the newsletter and asked them to keep praying for us. She said, "I feel in my spirit Rog you are not to send it, that God is doing something amazing. Leave it to Him." Well that shot me down in flames! I sat writing this part of the book while I fight disobedience. "What's wrong with asking friends and long term supporters for help?" "If God wants them to know He will tell them" she said. So that looks like a newsletter that will never be sent but watch this space!!

Coffee time:- Amanda came in for coffee. In the course of our conversation we were talking about the Bible. There were many conversations at that time and often in front of non-believers, so it was a ministry on its own. Amanda mentioned that she had been thinking about me that morning as she read Proverbs 16:3, so I looked it up. It was a verse that had been given to us many years ago *"Commit to the Lord whatever you do and your plans will succeed." (NIV)*

After coffee that led me to find another verse from long ago Newsletter Number 3 February 1985. I needed to find it but did not know where it was so I phoned a friend, who was able to remind me, *"Unless the Lord builds the house they labour in vain that build it."* Psalm 127:1 (NIV)

Chapter 29

Two Choices

We all have two choices when things get tough. We can choose self-pity which leads to returning to our old ways. Even now I am glad there is not a bottle of whisky in the house. Or we can search for Jesus, hence all the books by my bed. Needless to say He is there all the time so when He feels far off, guess who moved?

At the end of 2019, my step mum became very frail needing lots of trips to hospital. Over Christmas she was deteriorating badly and died on 24th January 2020. By that time Covid had arrived, and little did we realise how our lives would be devastated in the next two years. We managed to get mum's funeral in before the first lockdown and although this sounds awful, we felt it a blessing, on her behalf that she did not have to suffer the restrictions and loneliness of the lockdown rules.

Potential buyers were still looking round the farm and we sold a field to a neighbour and then two fields to Betel, which satisfied the bank for a while.

The farm was always a strange shape and not really big enough to be a viable farm and too big to be an open farm. By splitting it up it left us with the farm house (The Croft) and our Granny Flat (The Paddocks). Our daughter Nicky, Mick and their family moved into The Croft on one side of our house and in March 2020 lockdown started.

We had to become 'bubbles', or small hubs of relatives ensuring that we didn't see anyone else. Our grandson Bradley has Downs Syndrome and being in Nicky's family was part of our bubble with very strict rules. Kelly, living in the village with Hayden and Daisy, eventually became part of our bubble too.

Up to that point I had mentally handled things quite well although selling the farm was still a big issue. However I lost the joy of working with DCM Night Shelter. With the new Covid regulations and because of my age I was no longer allowed to help. It was such a terrible shock. I felt I had lost almost everything I enjoyed, my hens, my students, the farm, and now the Night Shelter.

Overnight I began to feel my age and I lost interest in almost everything, had no motivation to do anything and depression started to set in, so I went back on the pills.

Even though I was aware that God had blessed us in so many ways, I still felt low. Counting my blessings I realised that mum was safely with her Saviour (the most important reason for you to know my Jesus), we did not have to move, and even though the farm was still for sale, we would still be able to keep our granny flat along with Nicky's house. Also a large part of our debts had been repaid, and our bubble included all of our younger grandchildren.

I began to develop a strong guilt complex knowing I should feel blessed but in reality I felt awful. I had spent all my working life helping broken people and sharing God's love, but I could no longer do that. In fact I couldn't help anyone. I had a huge hole in me.

I watched the news too much, saw so many people in need and I could not jump in and help. I kept coming up with ways to be helpful but was told I couldn't. I felt I was letting God down and started to drink. A whisky half way through the morning, followed by more, is not a good idea but all through this God just kept on loving me and in some strange way I felt He was holding my hand.

I stopped writing the book in early March 2021. It was another lockdown in the UK and I was totally weary in my mind and body. I had no doubt that God would never leave me. I prayed a lot but I just did not 'feel' Him close. Looking through my diaries, I could see all the wonderful things that had happened that I had not acknowledged were from God. How could I possibly expect people reading my experiences to want to meet my Jesus unless I saw Him there?

May 2021.

"Inviting Jesus to come into our life is not a free pass to a comfortable life but it is a passport to a new way of looking at things and realising that the God who created this world also created me - and you; that no matter what happens He is always there beside us even if we cannot see or feel Him. We can bask in that unconditional love. This love will always be there for us even if we choose not to receive it.

This is a broken world and sadly bad things do happen to good people but it's the certain knowledge of knowing God's presence and as the world becomes more broken we need to find my Jesus.

To consider facing things without Him is unthinkable to me. As the lockdown continued my mental health and anxiety deteriorate. I have fought my battles and seem to lose a lot of them, but I have also come to realise that this is the story all through the Bible. A lot of the Psalms are written by people who are depressed. "*Why are you so cast down oh my soul?*". Possibly the best example is the book of Job. I guess none of us can truly understand how a God who loves us so much could allow these things to happen to such a faithful man. It is well documented that he questioned God's love and that his friends felt sure he had done something wrong. But God has a bigger picture and the end of Job's life was better than the beginning.

Although we cannot 'see' God, He is there all the time. I am looking out of the window and seeing spring happening after a long, wet winter. This is an example for all to see but then there are the personal times too. When He appears in the form of a phone call, someone at the door, or something physical happens. He is always there.

I have read dozens of Christian books about amazing people and places but they all seem to have floated there; if there were any bad times they were skimmed over. However, I believe if this book is to have any value I must try to put into words some of the things that have happened to me over recent years and how I have not handled them well. I want to share my journey with all its high and lows, revealing my Jesus working constantly throughout my life.

I am so thankful for the success of 'Happy Hens' and the hundreds of broken young people who have passed through. I praise God for the honour of my MBE. But I also realise that God was there when it all crashed! I need to confess my handling of lockdown and how without my Jesus I would surely have been a suicide case or an alcoholic. It has taken me two months to start writing again."

Looking through my diary, I can see that there were and are so many little things that made life bearable. I prayed. I cried. I still had that big black empty hole in me, we had lost all Christian contact. Our church had started a YouTube recording on a Sunday which was a help but I just couldn't get my head around modern technology. I missed contact with people. Community!

Nevertheless, I never stopped reading my Bible and so in my diary, there are the following scriptures:-

30th January - We must pray bigger dreams

- "Be still and know that I am God
- Cast all your cares upon Him as He cares for you.
- He is the God of the impossible
- He will do more than you can ever hope or imagine.

- Trust in the Lord with all your heart and lean not on your own understanding.
- The Lord knows the way through the wilderness, all I have to do is follow."

Wow, that must have been a good day because two days later I read "Really struggling in my head over finances, equipment to sell, no-one working for me, I am so lonely" – and yet I still held that Hand.

In February, pubs and hotels were still open and we went to Lakelands, in Ambleside to stay in a flat. I was quite depressed and struggling but we decided to go to the Lakelands Christian Fellowship Church. Before the service had even started, the pastor felt in his spirit to share about the woman in the Bible who had been bleeding for ten years. She had to push through the crowd to reach Jesus and her faith healed her. "Is there someone here who wants to push through the crowd, something you need?" I knew it was me. I went forward and explained about the farm project, the lack of money and the death of my dear mum.

Two people prayed for me and then they called Beryl out and prayed for us both. *This is for you Roger – you must let go"* and then quoted "our verse" – *"I know the plans I have for you declares the Lord, plans to prosper you and not to harm you, to give you a hope and a future – the project will not close down but others will run it, I am going to do a new thing."* Jeremiah 29:11 (NIV)

How many times have I been told to let go – but how? The place still needs looking after even if it's for sale.

This was a spectacular example of how even in a strange place God can reach out to you but you must make the first move and ask Him. We decided to go to church that day, we didn't have to and quite frankly we didn't want to but we did. We do not know the future but we know who does

7th February - "Real bad day in my head!! Will I ever learn?"

Little did we know that the eventual owners of the farm had been to look round the farm before Christmas. Their daughter had recently had a birthday party here and they had fallen in love with the place. But through February I was in a bad place, simply not trusting in all the scriptures I kept quoting to myself.

On the bright side, Beryl was doing all the things she had longed to do, particularly spending time with the grandchildren. Sadly, I was not much help with this (grumpy granddad!), baking, and cleaning (the house was spotless and I was constantly in trouble) but we did start to spend time with a lifelong couple. Sadly, Stuart had developed dementia and Sylvia was at her wits end so we started taking them out for lunch each week. That became the high spot of my week – How wonderful it is to give. How like Jesus.

Then I started 'The Chapel on the Bridge'. I have always got a Bible in my pocket to give away. Of course that had had to stop. However, I had an idea. Running past our farm is an old railway track converted to a footpath and it goes over Heage Lane just below our farm. I decided to put a waterproof plastic box full of New Testaments and Hope magazines on the bridge. I went up there every few days for a pray and to replenish the Bibles – it has a varied story.

Over two hundred Bibles were taken but on one occasion I found the lid broken and the Bibles and magazines thrown over the wall onto the road below. At that time, the road under the bridge was flooded and the Bibles were floating in the water. We replaced the box and restocked but sometime later we found someone had tried to set fire to the Bibles. (they don't burn very well) Rather than be put off we simply replaced everything.

I was very conscious of the testimony of that plastic box. Over two hundred Bibles had been taken but hundreds of people had seen it, had seen it destroyed, restored, and replaced – a living picture of Jesus! I felt I was beginning to fill my black empty hole.

Again from my diary and probably from the 'Word for Today', I write:-

- "Identify the enemy, probably doubt and fear
- Admit my own inadequacy
- Take the problem to the Lord
- Relax in faith
- Stand firm
- Thank God in advance"

Are you beginning to understand why I want you to meet my Jesus? Through all my darkest most apparently hopeless days I had to remember He was there. Again I think of the picture of God and Adam painted on the ceiling of the Sistine Chapel in Italy. God reaching out with His arm extended and His finger straight. While Adam lays back relaxed, his arm not quite straight, his finger bent, and the tiny gap between the tip of God's finger and the tip of Adam's finger.

In early March 2020 - "The 'Word for Today' reads – *'I will not be afraid and I will not be terrified of the future as Jehovah is looking after me."* How often do we read or say something that we do not really believe? I had to believe what I had just read.

I WILL BELIEVE. I stopped taking the pills that day! I offer caution here – Doctors and their prescription of the right pills are a gift from God and so often are a part of God's answer to prayer, but on occasions, and for me this was the first time. He says, *"I will heal you."* I did incidentally let my doctor know I had stopped in March and the reason why.

I Want You to Meet My Jesus

Chapter 30

High Spots

God is so good at encouraging – Happy Hens closed down a while ago and the electrician who had kept everything going for us over the years phoned just to find out how we were - that really blessed us - but as we said goodbye he said, "I have still got the Bible you gave me." Despite the lockdown, we Gideons (now "Good News For Everyone") have left an endless trail of good news and blessings that started for me over fifty years ago in that Hotel in Yorkshire.

Through all that time God was with me every step of the way. I repeatedly let Him down and cried a lot of tears, but I had to accept the fact that the past was past.

Beryl was different. She did all the things she had been unable to do whilst Happy Hens was happening - sewing, baking, looking after the grandchildren, and then she became a church leader. Forgive me but I was seriously jealous of her nonetheless I promised to support her. That has taken a lot of grace as my days were terribly empty and I had no enthusiasm to do anything. But God was faithfully dealing with me. I needed to rest; I needed to be empty and willing to change but did not feel able to commit myself to anything. Before lockdown, I was a relatively fit oldish person but after lockdown, I felt too old for anything.

Together we reinvented 'Monday Club' at church with a community meal delivered once a month during the lockdown, and after the lockdown, we continued it at the church to encourage people back to meeting together in the building.

We had a speaker come to the church from the Zambezi Mission. He suggested our church might like to sponsor a goat for a church in Malawi. I gave him £15 but phoned him later as I felt one goat was not much help. A nanny goat needed a Billy. So I suggested that we should start a goat project. We raised over £1,000, enough for over sixty goats. Enough goats for more than one church!

Then a friend of mine shared with me his work in Burundi. They were looking for people to go out and teach farming. My excuse of being too old was getting thin so Beryl and I went to see him and pray with him. He said to me "You are definitely not too old. For starters will you design a 500 bird free range chicken unit for the church in Burundi?"

After a time of prayer he had a picture for me. It was a clean sheet of paper, no marks, no creases, a perfectly clean sheet of A4 paper.

Watch this space!

I Want You to Meet My Jesus

Chapter 31

Tears

The word 'tears' conjures up in my mind a picture of a small child with grazed knees or a hungry baby. As adults, it is not the 'done thing' unless it is a special occasion like a funeral, or we may even cry happy tears at a wedding. Certainly, for us chaps it is definitely 'not on', and even on special occasions, we swallow like mad to keep the tears back in case someone sees them.

I have come to realise that tears are a gift of the Spirit. We feel we want to cry when we have reached the limit of our endurance of spiritual pain, unhappiness, or joy. I have often felt sorry for someone but only recently has that sorrow been so deep that I have wanted to cry. We realise that our world is in a mess and full of pain. Does that hurt enough to cry for?

A really angry lad came to us once and after a really bad argument one evening he stormed out of the house. I left him for a while before going off to look for him and found him with his arms around a calf's neck. He was crying and telling that calf everything that hurt inside. One day I had to take this same lad to his mum's house for some things. When mum saw him on the doorstep she shouted "What the f'in hell are you doing here? You know I don't want you." Can you imagine the damage that did to that teenage child? Beryl and I could understand his anger and his need to cry.

I also remember that I had a terrible row with the same young lad. He had been with us on and off for four years. On one occasion he went for me but my daughter got in the way. He stormed out of the house and kicked the dog on the way out. The dog was found cowering in the corner of the washhouse whining with a broken leg. This was pure anger let loose.

Two other lads went off down the drive after the lad, while I picked up the dog and carried him into the kitchen where stood Beryl with a teenage girl who was visiting. The girl insisted that we went straight to the vet but Beryl laid the dog on the floor, put her hands on him, and said, "Dear Jesus please make Sam better." To her complete amazement (and everyone else's) Sam licked her face, got up, and walked off as if nothing had happened.

Although we realised a miracle had happened we were all too shocked about the whole affair to take it all in. The pain we felt for the lad was intense but still not enough to make us cry for him. I looked at Beryl and said, "Why aren't you crying?" I was really needing an excuse to open the floodgate myself.

I had managed to get a message to the lad that the dog's leg was healed and two days later on Mothering Sunday there arrived a beautiful carnation for Beryl and a carefully selected card with a little note for me as well. It read, "Dear Roger – I thought I would reply to your letter, just to say thanks for the last four years, I hope they will not be wasted. Thank Beryl and God for me for mending the dog's leg. What I did was stupid. Maybe in a few months if I sort myself out we will learn to love each other again.

Love Rob

PS I did not say that all you have said to me in the past were lies. I know they weren't and maybe one day I will give you that letter back – I hope so."

Update 2022: Rob is now a very successful married businessman.

On the way to church that day I realised that it is only when we get to tears that we have gone as far as we can go and that is what God is waiting for. Not just mild interest or "I will pray for you" but real heartfelt tears of pain or joy. Only then He can go as far as He can and pour out all His blessings on us and through us.

Even as I realised this I was still swallowing hard in case the family thought I was cracking up – aren't we humans foolish? It's like going to the dentist, we know it's going to hurt; we know the pain will go afterward but given the choice, we will often avoid the dentist and keep the pain. Or ripping a plaster off hurts a bit more but it is over quickly. Here I was longing to cry, knowing that God wanted me to and would bless me, but still, my hang-ups got in the way.

I wrote these notes as a real beginner because I have still not let those tears go but I know that when I do God has taken me where He can really use me. As I copy these notes in 2022 I should add that I have a lovely friend at church who had no problem crying and I soon learnt from him.

2022

Today I am reminded that through my worst times of selling the farm and lockdown I read Psalm 40 hundreds of times.

"I waited patiently for the Lord
He turned to me and heard my cry

He lifted me up out of the mud and the mire
And set my feet on a rock
And gave me a firm place to stand
He put a new song in my mouth
A hymn of Praise to my God."
Psalm 40:1-3a (NIV)

I Want You to Meet My Jesus

Chapter 32

He Will Never Let You Down

The day after we were baptised all those years ago, I had the most awful backache for a few days, but through that experience, I discovered that our bodies, 'the packing case' can be hurt and even killed, but our spirits are separate and untouchable and that when we become born again they cannot be damaged in any way. For the non-Christian this is the part of us that is starved and hurting; that is how the devil would have it be. As our spirit suffers doctors are baffled by apparent mental disorders that are untreatable in medical terms. I firmly believe the Word (The Bible) is the food of the spirit and as we learn more of God our Creator so our spirit becomes stronger and in turn, our minds become healthier.

I relate an experience that happened to me and prompted me to write this chapter. Starting in November 1986 I had a swollen knee. Once or twice I asked for prayer and received a little relief but the pain continued and so I went to the Doctor who gave me some painkillers. In February 1987 there was no improvement so more pills were prescribed. Again no relief, in fact, the pain was now centred in a bone behind my kneecap and was spreading toward my ankle and up to my hip. So it was decided I should go to the hospital and see a bone specialist.

On the Saturday night before my visit, I could not sleep and started to really panic. "Cancer in the bones?" I thought. Then I thought I would have to have my leg amputated and needless to say, I did not find that idea attractive. So I laid in bed and prayed. I wanted to pray that my leg would get better but could only remember my Lord's words "*My Father if it is possible may this cup be taken from me yet not as I will but You will.*" Matthew 26:39(NIV)

As I prayed these words I realised that maybe peoples' lives would be challenged and changed if these things happened to me. I even listed some names of people I knew who stubbornly would not listen to God's message and yet could not fail to see Him working in my life if I retained my peace regardless of what happened. Did I love these people enough to lose my leg? Sounds a bit dramatic but that is how I saw it. I knew I was born again and that my spirit was indestructible, I knew that I wanted these people to find my Jesus in their lives, and so by the time

I went to sleep, I could almost look forward to whatever would happen. In fact, I had found peace in the situation.

The next morning I phoned our pastor and asked for prayer in the morning service. During the service, the pastor and the elders laid hands on me and prayed that my leg would be healed and that the doctor would be confounded. While they were praying my knee began to throb like mad. I relaxed and received whatever God had in store for me and the pain left.

Well, I made my visit to the bone specialist two days later and my knee was x-rayed. The pictures showed that I had osteoarthritis and that the back of my kneecap was rough, but still, there was no pain, just a bit of swelling. The specialist did his best to make it hurt, he twisted and pulled but the only time I yelled was when he dug his elbow into my thigh to get a better twist. He told me the only cure was to have my kneecap removed but as it did not hurt then, of course, that would not be necessary at this time. I was reminded of my pastor's prayer, that the doctor would be confounded.

I did in fact have a knee replacement twenty-five years later.

I Want You to Meet My Jesus

Chapter 33

The Farm is Sold.

Back to selling the farm

A couple came several times to the farm and were ready to make a serious offer. Our agent did a search and discovered they had run a brothel in Birmingham (imagine a brothel next to Betel, the Christian rehab in the middle of the farm!!) Then there was a single lady, very gushing and enthusiastic.

We walked around the farm and went into the kitchen for a cup of tea to discuss money. This was it at last!! Then the phone rang. It was our agent to book a viewing. The phone was on loudspeaker and I told him about the lady sitting next to me and he exploded "Oh no not Mrs ****! Get rid of her and I will explain later!" And he put the phone down. Well of course Mrs**** heard the conversation, went very red in the face, and departed!!

I phoned the agent back and apparently; this lady was known for running scams to borrow money to purchase properties and then disappears with the money just before completion. The police came to see us for a statement and she is now in prison. That's what I call the Lord's protection!

We had begun to meet with the potential new owners of the farm. They were not sure what they were going to do with it but they just loved it. As it was still in the middle of lockdown, contact with the Solicitor and the Estate Agent was a nightmare, with everyone working from home.

Although our prospective buyers had the money, wherever it was coming from was not happy about the portacabins, and so a line was drawn around the bungalow and the buildings, which again due to lockdown was just awful and everyone was getting frustrated and angry. They nearly pulled out several times but we all hung in there. The price was reduced and the sale finally went through on 28th August 2020. There are no words to describe what went on in my head through that time but there were many instances when I felt God's presence and protection.

The original sale would have included our house and the granny flat but after months of prayer and the decision to break it up our debts were paid. I can cheerfully say that we have kept our home and Nicky and her family are living next door. Nicky is working on our paddock with youngsters who have special needs, with rabbits, guinea pigs, pygmy goats, pigs, and chickens. She has picked up on our vision and is giving hope to some very special people.

Entries from my diary at that time are full of amazing stuff. Miracles! - lots of examples of how God has a bigger picture than we have.

When I look back over my diary entries for 2019 -2021 most of my days start with "I am having a bad day in my head and I don't want to get out of bed." I have recorded all the problems that needed to be resolved but also acknowledged that God has been faithful and that every problem was sorted by big and small miracles. So many big things were happening to me and I kept getting *"TRUST ME ROG".*

At the end of 2019 we had contact with a young person from many years ago who had recently gone to prison for murder and I kept in touch with him. He got on well with the chaplain and acknowledges that he wished he had listened to his mum and me many years ago but has now given his life to Jesus.

In one of my letters to him I told him I was having a problem getting up in the morning. His reply was "You know what Rog; I don't have to ask God to get me out of bed in the morning. He is the reason I get up." WOW! Good advice from the most unexpected source and a seed sown many years ago has germinated.

It is sad that God has done so much for me this year yet I feel so guilty and sorry for myself. His Love is so permanent and unconditional. I keep being told that my feelings are quite normal and not to beat myself up. *"If you focus on your pain you forget ME"*.

My thoughts turn to thousands of youngsters who have had severe problems over the lockdown, some more serious than others.

One of our precious grandsons, whose parents had recently split up, really struggled, and started cutting himself. Then he started running away and threatening to kill himself. We had to involve the police I believe about six times. The prayer chain was motivated each time and he was found but the last one I will never forget. He texted his social worker that he had a rope around his neck and all he had to do was jump.

The police were already on the scene but suddenly we had eight police cars, a dog, a drone, and a helicopter. The drone found him in the pitch dark running towards the river. The drone directed the helicopter and with a huge light directed the swarm of police on the ground who finally caught up with him and pulled him out of the river with a rope around his neck

MIRACLE ONE

A picture I will never forget is of my grandson wet and muddy handcuffed to a policeman. He was then taken off to the hospital. We asked if he could be kept in but there was nowhere in Derbyshire that could take him, so he went home after a night in the hospital. Nothing had changed and then he developed a violent tic. His mum was so stressed and afraid she brought him up to us. We prayed with him and the violence stopped and was completely gone by the next morning.

MIRACLE TWO

If he had been found a place when we asked he would probably have gone into care. As it was he ended up with us, his family, being loved and prayed for.

MIRACLE THREE

His Healing.

He was soon back to school but sadly that was not the end of it and the school could not keep him safe. On one occasion he ran away and ended up in a lake. A teacher followed him in and had to drag him out. There was a zoom meeting with the school, social worker, his mum, and him. Our lack of faith expected him to do his worst but he came into the room with his uniform on and said "I am not the boy who left school last July, I have changed. I know I have a lot of catching up to do and I will." Well, we were all speechless.

Now as I write in March 2022 he is getting back to school, has passed his mock exams, and has been accepted for college in September.

The moral of this story is that God never left us and that prayer moves mountains.

How important it is for you to get to know 'My Jesus?'

February 2022 - I came out of lockdown a very different person. Very confused! I have always worked with broken people but for two years I have done nothing. I was out of condition mentally, physically, and spiritually, my days were empty, I needed something to get out of bed for but I felt so lazy.

Lockdown had come at a terrible time for me as it coincided with mum dying, selling the farm, my retirement, and losing all the things I really enjoyed doing "Dear God please give me something to do, give me a ministry."

Chapter 34

The End

Well, that's it 1984 - 2022. This has been a very practical story because we have a very practical God who sent His Son down to earth to set us all free, to forgive us our sins, and to grant us eternity with Him.

We are getting towards the end of the book now. It has been strange reading through my notes and diaries that I wrote over the last few decades. Looking back to 1987 I see at that time that God seemed to explain things to me and I was hungry to learn. I expected Miracles. What happened to me? I feel I was a better Christian then than now. I had more faith. So this has been a refreshing journey for me as I rewrite those notes word for word. Maybe I am more mature now.

The end, the beginning, or somewhere in the middle. That seems a very indecisive title for the last part of the book, but which is it?

1987 I write - It is the end of the needs concerning the restoration of both barns and it is the fruit of the faith that has been put into it, but I believe the greatest job has just begun. The prayer and faith that has gotten us this far has only prepared us for the work ahead. In physical terms, the barn needs to be maintained, in financial terms it has to be heated, and the people who use it need to be fed. But even greater than that they need to be loved. And all of those who run the barn must be lifted up in prayer in a very special way to claim victory over the enemy in those damaged lives. To those who have been with us so far thank you, to those who are to be added to us or replace us through His calling, we look forward with great joy to meeting with you and watching with you so that we can all share in the tremendous blessings that come from serving Him.

This was written many years ago when none of the barns had a roof. Now for over twenty years, it has been run by Betel. Through them, ALL of the above needs and prayers have been met – Isn't God good! A school for evangelism!!! Ten baptisms and two weddings in the past year. WOW!)

When I started writing this book I prayed that through it people would wish to find my Jesus in their lives. Even as I write this I feel a great joy inside of me that God has used my life in this way.

Learning to pray bigger prayers and expecting answers.

This book has been about my relationship with Jesus but recently through lockdown, I have learned to pray bigger prayers for the world. I used to think that was such a waste of time. What difference could my prayers possibly make? But God gave me two pictures, one of a bale of hay, and reminded me that that bale of hay is made up of thousands of blades of grass. Likewise, the second picture was of a bushel of wheat that is made of thousands of single grains. So I find I have been able to pray about Covid in a much broader way. As I write Russia is invading Ukraine with a real possibility of war in Europe and so I pray to my Jesus.

The Challenge

They've been blamed for doing this
And blamed for doing that
And someone out there probably thinks
They've challenged the Preacher's cat.

But all that has been spoken
And all that has been done
Was not by the man who said it
 But by the leading of God's Son.

So if you have been challenged
Or hurt in any way
Before you get all angry
 Just stop a while and pray.

God doesn't want to hurt us
Each one of us knows that
He only wants to lead us
And knows just where we are at.

The bit of us that's selfish
The bit of us that's wrong
Will just keep on hurting
Till we've given it to God's Son.

The End

So thank the man who spoke the word
That made you stop and think
The Lord used him to save your life
If you went away to think.

I Want You to Meet My Jesus

Chapter 35

Just for You ~ Psalm 23(NIV)

If you have decided to start searching for your Jesus I would like to close the book by sharing notes and verses that have helped me and are very precious to me, so this last part is just for you.

Some years ago when I was very troubled, and all things seemed to be getting on top of me, I did not know which way to turn or what decisions to take. A friend suggested that I should go and read Psalm 23 and allow it to become real to me.

I had not been born again then but I read it and it really blessed me, as the Word of God will, if we read it willingly, and hungrily seeking guidance and comfort. But now sometime later I still find that when all things seem tangled then I must take time out to pray and find peace. It is hard to do anything or even pray rationally from a troubled heart. We make wrong, unthought-through decisions, or we pray pleading prayers wanting our answers. It is not easy, but God will give us that peace even when our business has just gone wrong, our home is broken for one reason or another or a loved one has just died. But as we learn more about our Loving Heavenly Father, so we also know that He will lead us through these situations. We can learn and be strengthened by them and so no matter how bad things seem at times let my interpretations comfort you and encourage you:

"The Lord is my Shepherd"

That conjures up a picture of protection. There will always be sheep in any flock that strays or gets tangled up in something. The shepherd is watching and waiting to retrieve that sheep. Very few are willing and struggle; some do actually manage to run off and are not seen again but the fact is the shepherd desires to rescue them all.

"I shall not be in want"

In all my times of deepest trouble or despair, I have come to God with a shopping list of what I want to put the situation right as I see it. But as I read this line I discover that I really do have everything I NEED even in my darkest moments. There are lots more things that I would like to have but that is different. To God, at that time it is unnecessary for me to have them.

"He makes me lie down in green pastures"

Like so many other things 'He lets us' but do we do it? If we are not careful we become addicted to doing something. If there are lots of jobs to do we find it difficult, or even a waste of time to sit down and pray. Some say they can pray whilst they are working and that is great but we must take time out so, that our entire concentration is centred on prayer, as our spirits listen for answers. Even now in 2022 I still find it difficult to hear.

"He leads beside quiet waters"

Not wet water but a cool refreshing feeling that will refresh and heal our inner hurting self. This can only happen from willingly resting in Him. If we struggle and give up we will not find that peace, and so will not experience that refreshing – so keep trying. All these things come from our willingness to put God first.

"He restores my soul"

After His refreshing and our healing we will receive renewed strength and spiritual insight to cope with whatever brought us down.

"He guides me in paths of righteousness for His names sake"

I understand that in the Bible there are 8,000 promises for each one of us. Why are we so frightened to come to My Jesus? This is just one of those 8,000 promises but He can only guide us if we are willing to learn and to listen.

"Even if I walk through the valley of the shadow of death I will fear no evil"

Things will happen to us and in this world full of selfishness and violence those things can cause even the most faithful of Christians to feel they are in the darkness. But in this darkness, there is a pinpoint of light we can follow. Can you see that light? If not you may be lost in despair. All you need is to believe that Jesus died for you, that His Father is your Father and that He is your shepherd. You will be able to see the light and be saved.

"For you are with me
Your rod and staff they comfort me
You prepare a table before me
In the presence of my enemies
You anoint my head with oil
My cup overflows"

This is surely the most wonderful promise of things for now and to come after our earthly bodies have passed away and we receive the final glory of being born again and filled with the Spirit of Jesus. Whatever our suffering appears to be here on earth it is only a very short time in comparison to eternity, and this verse tells us what eternity will be like. Sometimes I just can't wait!

"Surely goodness and love will follow me all the days of my life"

But meanwhile, we are here on earth to love our neighbours, to seek out and save the lost sheep, and to spread the good news, and His goodness and love will never leave us.

"And I will dwell in the house of the Lord forever."

No matter how bad things are or seem to be, Jesus can change any life if He is invited to, all you need to do is ask Him.

God Bless you.

22nd June 2022

When I wrote the date, 22nd June 2022, I thought that I had finished but then a few days later I found a crumpled piece of paper behind a pile of books. It was not dated but must have been written in one of my many darkest hours when Happy Hens had closed, the farm was for sale, and all these circumstances mixed with lockdown, but what an amazing last paragraph to this book:-

"And Jesus looked over my shoulder and asked, *"What do you want?"*

I simply sat and prayed and asked what it means, to sit and let your mind wander and capture the meaning that becomes clear "What do I want?"

"I want peace, for my mind to be free from torment, to be able to think clearly, and for God to help me in my decisions. I want Jesus to walk with me and comfort me when I am struggling, I want Him to help me to be a good person, a consistent caring person, and a loving person."

Now several years later I find that piece of paper and every part of that cry for help has been answered. WOW, that's my Jesus!

27th June 2022 - "Please God take my life and show me how to live my days for you." God reminded me of the ministry He gave us so many years ago, to love the unlovable. Despite all that we have 'lost' or passed on over recent years, which is still our Ministry. "Oh Lord help us to be a blessing machine."

I Want You to Meet My Jesus

Betel Testimonies

Holly

"Nothing could satisfy. Something was always missing.

Smoking and drinking from a very early age I continued this lifestyle through my schooling years as I prepared to become a dental nurse. Drinking and clubbing every weekend turned into drinking every day. In my early twenties in a space of just a few weeks, I lost everything, my home, my job, and my driving license. My friends and family wanted nothing to do with me because of the excessive drinking. Given an ultimatum of prison or Betel in Etwall, I chose the latter.

In coming to Betel in 2016 I felt an overwhelming sense of peace and that this place was my home. I didn't know Jesus but my leader Jan did. I saw something in her that I desperately wanted.

That one thing was Jesus. Jan's example of Christ in her led me to want that life of restoration and hope.

Over time I had a full restoration with family and friends; the relationships I have now are better than they were before. I have had healing in my heart and life; the Lord has taken me on a journey of transformation and change.

I have had the wonderful opportunity to become a women's leader in Betel helping and serving others. I met my husband Max in Betel; we have been married for three years and serve alongside Sam and Karen at Betel Derby (Etwall). I would not change my life now. I love to serve in our community amongst friends. God, and Him using the vessel of Betel, has transformed my life."

Ryan

"My name is Ryan Morris; I am from a town in the North West of Manchester called Leigh.

As a child, I had what you call a normal life, loving parents who provided everything I needed, a brother whom I looked up to, and a sister I loved very much.

When I was 13 years old I started to get into drugs and drinking which very quickly spiralled out of control and over the next 18 years my life consisted of taking heroin and crack which led to a life of crime and as a result, I served several prison sentences. I was never able to hold a job down and burnt many bridges with my family and friends; I had finally reached a place of destruction and loss of any hope for my life.

One day I was shoplifting in Leigh town centre to feed my habit and walked into a charity shop called 'Heaven Scent'. The owner of the shop was a man called John Shipton. I couldn't bring myself to steal from this man whom I had become friendly with. John told me about a place where I could get some help, it was called Betel. I told him I had tried 'rehab' many times without any success and didn't believe that this place was any different to the others I had tried. "But this place is different!!"

How right he was!!

I arrived at Betel Derby (Etwall) on 5th January 2017. I looked awful; I was grey and weak and very fragile. I instantly sensed that there was something different about this place. People greeted me and made me feel welcome, making me feel that everything will be OK. The men around me who had been addicts themselves were asking me if there was anything I needed; they really cared and I hadn't felt that for such a long time. I was broken and hurting and people wanted to help me. The love I received was undeniable and I felt such a strong sense of peace.

God has fully restored my relationships with my family and they have seen such a change in me.

He has restored my mental and physical health. There are so many new skills I have learnt and I am using them to lead and help run the gardens business which funds the charity. We also have a furniture business that doesn't only restore furniture it helps to restore broken lives.

Betel is a very special place and God uses it to change lives on a daily basis.

If I hadn't gone to Betel when I did I would have been dead by now, if not sooner. The day I arrived there was the day God stepped in and saved my life, transformed my very being, and showed me how to love as He loves and for that, I am eternally grateful.

"Here is a trustworthy saying that deserves full acceptance. Christ came into the world to save sinners, of whom I am the worst." 1 Timothy 1:15 (NIV)

When I read Ryan's testimony my bottom jaw dropped. John Shipton had been a major part of my life in the 1980s - a cattle dealer living in a caravan, almost the last person I would have expected to become a Christian. The Bible says that no seed is wasted. Not only had John given his life to the Lord but he in turn had witnessed to others. I wonder how many others he had taken to Betel. I understand that he passed away two years ago.

About the Author

Roger Hosking along with His loving wife Beryl founded and ran 'Happy Hens' for many years serving as the hand and feet of Jesus to many young people who were to experience the unconditional love of God first hand.

Roger received recognition for this in 2011 receiving an MBE for His commitment to working with many young people and the great work they achieved, as God used both Roger and his wife to touch and offer a second chance to so many young lives.

If you would like to get in touch with Roger his e-mail address is rogerhosking2@gmail.com.

Printed in Great Britain
by Amazon